A Tiny Introduction to JavaScript
with Exercises and Puzzles

by Matthew MacDonald

A Tiny Introduction to JavaScript with Exercises and Puzzles

Copyright © 2020 by Matthew MacDonald. All rights reserved.

This book or any portion of it may not be reproduced or used in any manner without the express written permission of the publisher.

Published by ProseTech
Toronto, Ontario

To learn more about our publishing projects, visit http://prosetech.com

To contact the author, email matthew@prosetech.com

November 2020:   First Edition

ISBN-13: 978-1-7753737-6-6

Contents

Welcome 9
    What you need to use this guide 10
    Why JavaScript? 10
    Why CodePen? 11
    What if I'm actually an adult? 11
    About me 12
    How can I support the Tiny Introductions project? 12

Chapter Zero: CodePen: Your New Home 13
    Signing up on CodePen 13
    Looking at an example on CodePen 13
    Hiding the CSS 16
    Seeing a bigger preview 16
    Forking an example 18
    Turning on autocomplete 20
    What comes after CodePen 21

Chapter 1: What JavaScript Looks Like 23
    Statements 23
    Comments 25
    Blocks and functions 26
    Try it yourself! Hello, Wizard 28
    Optional Really big comments 29

Chapter 2: How Events Work 31

A really quick HTML review 31

How events work 32

Try it yourself! The Staggering Page of Heartbreaking Events 34

Try it yourself! The Broken Button 35

Chapter 3: Storing Information in Variables 37

Declaring a variable 37

Putting a value in a variable 38

Using numbers and text 40

Try it yourself! Predict the Future 41

Optional Putting quotation marks in a string 41

Good variable names 42

Try it yourself! Hello, Ninja 43

Variables that don't exist 43

Try it yourself! Find the Impostor 44

Optional Using TypeScript error checking 47

Copying variables 48

Try it yourself! The Gift Swapper 49

Chapter 4: Changing Variables 51

Really easy math 51

Slightly fancier math 52

Try it yourself! Pocket Calculator 53

Calculations with variables 53

Try it yourself! Pocket Calculator II 55

Calculations can go anywhere 56

Really easy "math" with text 57

Adding numbers and text together 58

Try it yourself! Alice the Unshakeable 59

    Optional Variables that never change 60

Chapter 5: Interacting with the Page 63

    Introducing the DOM 63

    Getting information out of a text box 64

    Try it yourself! A Greeting from the King 67

    Converting strings to numbers 68

    Try it yourself! Broken Adder 69

    Showing a message in the page 69

    Try it yourself! A Greeting from the King Rebooted 71

    Optional Changing a picture 71

Chapter 6: The Lifetime of a Variable 73

    Local variables 73

    Global variables 74

    Sharing the same variable with different functions 75

    Try it yourself! The Friendly Angry Ogre 77

    Try it yourself! The Broken Jellybean Counter 78

    The secret of the braces 79

    Wise advice about global variables 79

Chapter 7: Making Decisions 81

    Introducing conditions 81

    The if statement 82

    More logical operators 84

    Try it yourself! The Bowl of Beans 86

    The else block 87

    Try it yourself! The Bowl of Beans Improved 88

    Conditional logic with unlimited possibilities 88

    Try it yourself! Predict the Future 90

Try it yourself! Beans Ain't Free 92

Chapter 8: More Decision Making 93

Combining two conditions (using 'and') 93

Combining two conditions (using 'or') 95

Try it yourself! Predict the Future 96

The switch statement 97

Try it yourself! The Goblin Dice Gambler 100

Chapter 9: Repeating Yourself with Loops 103

The simplest possible loop 103

A loop that counts 104

Try it yourself! Predict the Future 106

Try it yourself! Put It In Reverse 106

Putting the condition at the end 107

A loop without a counter 109

Try it yourself! Million Dollar Pizza 110

Try it yourself! Million Dollar Pizza II 112

Optional For, a loop with a built-in counter 113

Chapter 10: Organizing with Functions 115

Adding new functions 115

Calling a function 116

Try it yourself! Follow the Function Trail 119

Functions that get data 119

Using multiple parameters 121

Try it yourself! Alien Language Translator 122

Chapter 11: Functions that Answer Questions 125

Functions that give answers 125

Try it yourself! Predict the Future 127

Try it yourself! Alien Language Translator II 128

Chapter 12: Getting More Serious with Math 131

Math shortcuts 131

Try it yourself! Predict the Future 133

The wacky mistake JavaScript makes with decimals 134

Try it yourself! The Broken Dime Adder 135

Peeking into the Math object 135

Try it yourself! How Big Is this Cake? 137

Rounding numbers 138

Try it yourself! How Big Is this Cake? (II) 140

Chapter 13: The Magic of Random Numbers 141

Random and pseudo-random 141

Generating random numbers 142

Try it yourself! Number Guesser of Doom 144

Try it yourself! Ice, Dagger, Lava 146

What Comes Next 149

Welcome

These days, you can't turn around twice without someone trying to teach you how to code. The world is full of websites, courses, books, and games that promise to introduce you to the magical art of computer programming.

So why did I write my own book?

When my daughters started learning to code, I discovered that most tutorials were as dry as dust. If you wanted something more fun, you could play a coding game and write commands to move a character around a maze (like a princess, a zombie, a turtle, whatever). But unlike real programming, there was no chance to be creative. There was no freedom. There was no invitation to build *your own* programs.

I wanted something different. Something...

- **Hands-on.** If you want to learn a new skill, you need to practice. Otherwise, it's just a bunch of theory swimming around in your head.
- **Friendly for beginners.** If you're a beginner, it's not enough to learn the basics of a programming language like JavaScript. You also need to learn the concepts of programming at the same time.
- **No setup required.** The world is full of amazing frameworks, tools, and code editors. But who wants to install a bunch of software before you even get started?
- **Tiny.** I'm a programming nerd, so I *like* talking about things like Big O notation. But no one needs to be buried in theory at the start of their journey. In this book, every chapter is a bite-sized lesson that you can usually finish in one sitting.
- **Kinda fun.** Not everyone has the motivation to learn from an old-fashioned textbook. But who doesn't want to play dice with a cheating goblin?

So I decided to make something of my own. Then I unleashed it on my family.

This is the result of those experiments.

What you need to use this guide

You need a computer. Any type will do. (Please don't try to learn to program on a smartphone.) You don't need to install any software, because you're going to write all your examples using the free CodePen website.

You do need to know a little bit about HTML. Web pages are written in HTML, and JavaScript lives in web pages. Most JavaScript code spends a lot of time interacting with a web page—for example, changing text on a page, reacting when buttons are clicked, and so on.

Trying to learn both JavaScript and HTML at once is a bit of a headache. But if you've never played around with HTML before, we have a solution. You can learn just enough to get by from the very short tutorial *Messing Up the Web* (available at http://tiny.cc/webmess). Complete that before you start this guide.

Why JavaScript?

JavaScript is a great first language for people learning to code. It's not because JavaScript is a great teaching language (it mostly isn't). It's because JavaScript is *everywhere*—on every operating system, every browser, and almost every electronic device that's more complicated than a toaster.

That means you can effortlessly share your JavaScript programs with friends. Unlike all the rest of computing history, there's no downloading, installing, or configuring. And it doesn't hurt that JavaScript syntax is similar to many other professional languages, like Java and C#. That means the effort you spend to learn JavaScript is never wasted.

Why CodePen?

CodePen is one of several free JavaScript playgrounds that you can use in your browser. With CodePen, you can write JavaScript code, test it, and save it for later, without needing to set anything up. And all the pieces of your solution—the HTML that creates the page, the CSS that makes it look good, and the JavaScript that powers it—are brought together in one place. There's no need to juggle separate files.

This guide uses CodePen for all its exercises. Usually, you'll start with a project that's already built, and then change it. Maybe you'll need to make an enhancement or fix a problem. And when you're finished, you can show your work to other people just by sending them a link.

What if I'm actually an adult?

Take comfort, it's not all bad. But if the question is "Can I use this book even if I'm not a kid?" then the answer is easy—*yes*!

However, this book assumes you're learning JavaScript and programming for the first time. If you already know a bit about programming, you'll probably prefer a guide that focuses on the JavaScript language without re-introducing the concepts you already know.

About me

I've written dozens of computer books for publishers like O'Reilly, Apress, No Starch, and McGraw Hill. Some of them are still helpfully propping open doors in my house.

These days I spend most of my time experimenting with weird projects and writing about the art of software building on Young Coder (http://medium.com/young-coder). Follow me there, or on Twitter (http://twitter.com/prosetech), or go to my website if you're curious about the things I've written in the past (http://prosetech.com).

How can I support the Tiny Introductions project?

Please enjoy this book guilt-free! Share it with your family! Give it to your friends! There's no limit, so long as you don't change it or pass it off as your own work.

If you find mistakes, please let me know. I greatly benefit from people pointing out problems I've missed, so they don't frustrate other readers. Send me your complaints, comments, questions, and suggestions to matthew@prosetech.com. What worked? What's still keeping you up at night? Don't be shy!

If you feel particularly enthusiastic about the Tiny Introductions project, and you want to say thanks (or just encourage me to write more books in the series), you can buy your own copy of *A Tiny Introduction to JavaScript*. It's available in print from Amazon (in which case I get a teeny portion of the proceeds) or in a pay-what-you-can PDF form on Gumroad. Thanks a bunch!

Chapter Zero

CodePen: Your New Home

All the work you'll do in this guide happens in CodePen. So before you get started, it's time to check out your new home.

CodePen is a JavaScript *playground*. That means it's a place where you can write web pages and try them out. CodePen isn't the only JavaScript playground, but it's my favorite. It's easy to use. You can start with someone else's example, change it, and save it to your own account. And all the basic features are free.

Signing up on CodePen

You don't need an account to use CodePen. But having an account is a good idea, because it allows you to save your work. CodePen accounts are free (although you can pay for a pro account with extra features).

To create a CodePen account, go to http://codepen.io and click the **Sign Up** button. You need to give your email address, choose a password, and pick a CodePen name. You know, the usual stuff. Or, you can register with a social media account that you already use, like Twitter or Facebook.

Looking at an example on CodePen

In this guide, you get links that take you to each example. Try it out now, by visiting *The Most Wonderful Button in the World*:

https://codepen.io/prosetech/pen/PoNqRbq

If you're reading this guide in a browser, here's a useful trick. Hold down the **Ctrl** key when you click the link. That way the example opens in a new tab, and doesn't take you away from what you're reading right here, in this tab.

> **NOTE** If you're reading this book on paper, you obviously can't click the links. To save yourself some typing, visit http://prosetech.com/tiny, where there's a list of all the examples, organized by chapter.

When you go to an example in CodePen, you'll see a window that's split into several parts.

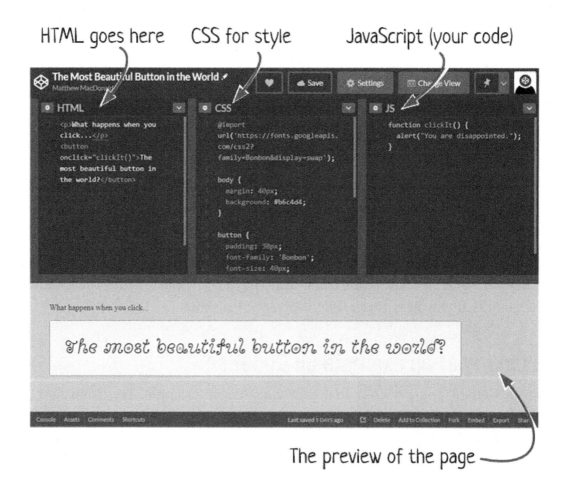

There are four boxes in the CodePen window:

- **HTML.** That's the content of your web page (the elements and text).
- **CSS.** These are the styles that set how your web page looks.
- **JavaScript.** This is the code you're going to learn to write. You'll spend a lot of time in this box.
- **Preview.** This is what the actual page you're building looks like (so far).

Usually, the HTML, CSS, and JavaScript sections are arranged on the top, and the preview is underneath.

If your browser window is too small, CodePen rearranges itself to put the preview on the right side, and combines the HTML, CSS, and JavaScript sections on the left.

You can start changing a CodePen example right away. Try it out with *The Most Wonderful Button in the World*. Click in the HTML box, and change the text on the button. (Right now, it's "The most beautiful button in the world?") A moment after your change, the preview will update itself. If you're noticing a delay, you can always click the preview section to hurry it up.

> **NOTE** Remember, if you don't know anything about HTML and you aren't comfortable editing it yet, you can read the *Messing Up the Web* tutorial to get started (http://tiny.cc/webmess).

Hiding the CSS

CSS (Cascading Style Sheets) is the standard you use to format the appearance of a web page. All the examples you'll see in this guide have some formatting. But if you don't want to be distracted by that information (and you want more space to read your JavaScript code), you can temporarily hide the CSS section on CodePen.

To do that, click the tiny down-arrow button at the top of the CSS box and choose **Minimize CSS Editor**.

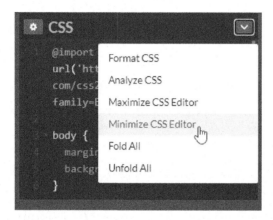

You can hide the other CodePen boxes, too, but you won't want to. You need to keep the HTML and JavaScript handy in order to finish each example.

Seeing a bigger preview

Sometimes CodePen tries to cram too much stuff into your web browser window. The web page preview (at the bottom) can be particularly awkward. It's not very tall, so you might need to scroll up and down to see the whole preview.

To improve this situation, you can resize different parts of the CodePen window. The trick is to click in between the boxes, on the black bars that separate each section. Then you can drag them to make a section smaller or bigger.

Sometimes, no matter what you do, you can't fit everything in at once. In this case, it's time to switch views using the **Change View** button (at the top right of the CodePen window). Click it and choose another option to take a different look at your example. Click **Full Page View** to temporarily expand the web page preview so it fills the whole window. Or, choose one of the other box arrangements under the **Editor Layout** heading to put the preview window on the side.

When you're in full page view, you can't see the other stuff, like your HTML and JavaScript. When it's time to switch back to normal so you can edit your example, click the **Change View** button again and choose **Editor View**. You'll get used to jumping back and forth in no time.

Forking an example

When you go to an example like *The Most Wonderful Button in the World*, you're seeing the version I created. You can make changes, but your changes are temporary. They won't replace my version.

Often, you'll want to save your work. Maybe you want to look at it later. Or maybe you're in the middle of a big change. Maybe you want to show it to someone else. In all of these cases, the solution is to *fork* the example, which means to create your own copy. (The word "fork" comes from a fork in the road—a place where the path splits. You're going to split the code and take your own path.)

To fork an example, you need to have a CodePen account. Assuming you have one, all you need to do is click the **Fork** button at the bottom of the window. The example is now yours to change however you want and save for the future.

The very tiny Fork button

When you fork an example, your name appears under the example name, which shows that you're the owner of this new copy. You can also rename the example, if you want. (To do that, click the pencil icon next to the name.)

More importantly, your new copy also gets a new web address.

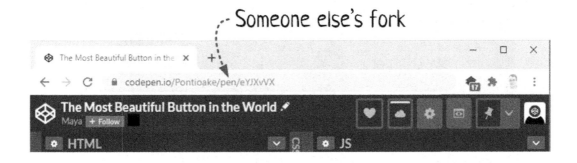

You use the new address whenever you need to see your version of the example. You can see all the examples you've saved (they're called *pens*) in your CodePen dashboard at https://codepen.io/dashboard.

Forking isn't the only way to make an example. You can also start writing an example from scratch. You might do this to follow along with some of the lessons in this guide, or just try out your own random ideas. To create a new, blank example, click the person picture in the top-right corner of the CodePen site and choose **New Pen**.

Turning on autocomplete

CodePen has a nifty feature called *autocomplete* that can give you suggestions while you type. For example, CodePen's autocomplete can suggest the name of certain code ingredients. (This will make more sense once you start learning JavaScript.)

The only problem with autocomplete is that you need to turn it on yourself. You should definitely do that before you get started learning JavaScript. Here's how:

1. Click the tiny person picture in the top-right corner of the CodePen site.
2. Click **Settings**.
3. Scroll down the page until you find the **Editor Options** box.
4. Make sure the **Autocomplete** setting is checked.

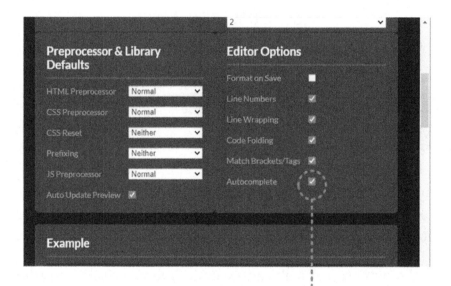

The Autocomplete checkbox

What comes after CodePen

Of course, just because you start in CodePen doesn't mean you have to stay there. Eventually you can take the code you've written, save it on your computer, and use a professional (but still free) editor like Visual Studio Code.

When you're ready to take this road, CodePen has an export feature that can help you out. Here's how to use it:

1. Click the **Export** button. (It's in the bottom-right corner of the window, near the tiny **Fork** button.)
2. Click **Export .zip** to create a zipped-up package with all the files you need (that includes the HTML, CSS, and JavaScript).
3. Click **Download .zip** to copy the ZIP file to your computer. Now you can open it, get the files, and edit them in a different editor.

But there's plenty of time for all that later. Right now, CodePen is the perfect place to get started with JavaScript.

Chapter 1
What JavaScript Looks Like

You're about to spend a lot of time looking at code. To help you find your way around, you need to get more familiar with the way JavaScript code is written.

These arcane rules are known to JavaScript wizards as *syntax*. Once you know some of the rules of JavaScript syntax, code will start looking a lot more like magic instructions and a lot less like complete gibberish.

Statements

When you look at a chunk of JavaScript code, you'll see a sequence of *statements*—basically, commands that tell your web browser to do something. Here's one now:

```
alert("Hi there!");
```

The `alert()` command is simple. It shows a small pop-up window with whatever message you want. (You put the message—like *Hi there!*—in quotation marks.) An alert box isn't the most polite way to get attention, but it works.

If you're completely new to JavaScript, you won't understand exactly how this command works, and that's OK. But you should notice that this command has a semicolon (;) at the end. Although semicolons aren't absolutely required in JavaScript, serious programmers always use them. They show where each code statement stops.

If you run out of room to comfortably fit a statement on one line, you can split it pretty much wherever you want, as long as you remember to end with the semicolon. Here's an example that shows the same message as before, but now puts the statement on two lines:

```
alert(
"Hi there!");
```

You can also add spaces to arrange your code:

```
    alert(
        "Hi there!");
```

It's still the same command. JavaScript ignores extra spaces, just like it ignores line breaks.

Of course, you can't do much with just one statement. Even a small program has a series of statements, one after the other. When a piece of JavaScript code is running, the browser goes through the statements one by one, triggering each command in order.

Comments

Statements that start with two forward slashes `//` are comments. JavaScript ignores all comments.

```
// I don't do anything at all!
```

You can add comments wherever you want. Often, you use a comment to explain what's about to happen in the next code statement:

```
// Show a message.
alert("Hi there!");
```

You can also use comments to point out an important section of code. Many of the tutorials in this guide have comments that tell you where to pay attention or what you need to change:

```
// This is where things go wrong.
```

You can also put the comment slashes in front of a code statement to temporarily turn it off. For example, this `alert()` command won't do anything because it's been changed into a comment:

```
//alert("Hi there!");
```

This trick is called *commenting out* code. You might use it instead of deleting a line of code if you think you'll need the code later.

> **TIP** In CodePen (and most other code editors), comments are shown in a different color than statements. That makes it easier to spot the code.

Blocks and functions

JavaScript uses curly brackets, called *braces*, to group together sections of code that have one or more statements. Each section starts with an opening brace:

```
{
```

And ends with a closing brace:

```
}
```

(If you're hunting for these symbols on the keyboard, you can usually get them by holding down **Shift** and typing the square **[ ]** brackets, which are just to the right of the **P** key.)

As you learn JavaScript, you'll see these braces used in different places. The first place you'll see them is in *functions*. You can think of a function as a small section of code that does one task. You can recognize a function because it starts with the word `function`. Here's a simple example:

```
function showMessage() {
    alert("Hi there!");
}
```

Every function has a name, which appears after the word `function` and before the parentheses ( ). The person who creates the function chooses the name. This function is named `showMessage`, and it contains just one statement.

Here's a slightly longer version of the showMessage() function. It holds two comments and two statements:

```
function showMessage() {
  // Show the first message.
  alert("Hi there!");

  // After you click OK, you get to see this bonus message.
  alert("It's me again!");
}
```

Here's exactly what happens when the code in this function runs:

1. JavaScript skips over the first comment (// Show the first ...)
2. The alert() function shows the first message in an alert box.
3. Now the code stops. It's waiting for someone to close the alert box.
4. When you click **OK**, JavaScript carries on.
5. JavaScript skips over the second comment (// After you click ...)
6. The alert() function shows the second message.
7. When you click **OK**, JavaScript carries on and the function ends. That's all for now.

There are a few other details you might notice here. For example, every line in this function is indented with two empty spaces. These spaces are totally optional, but it's one of the many ways that people make code easier to read and understand. And making code easier to understand becomes a Very Big Deal as your programs get more complex.

> **NOTE** For now, every code statement you write belongs inside a function. Don't put code above a function block, after a function block, or between two function blocks. (You can put comments there, though.)

Try it yourself!

▶ **Hello, Wizard? (Challenge Level: Easy)**

https://codepen.io/prosetech/pen/wvMjPbM

It's a common tradition to start learning a new programming language with something called a *Hello World* program. All a *Hello World* program does is display a message. It proves that your code is working—and that's it.

The *Hello, Wizard?* example is a slight variation on this idea. Right now, it shows a rather unpleasant message when you click the **Greet Me** button.

Here's what you need to do to correct it:

- Find the `showMessage()` function. That's the code that runs when you click the button. It's also the only code in this example.
- Deactivate the rude message by adding the comment slashes (`//`) in the right place. In other words, you're going to turn the bad `alert()` command into a harmless comment.

- Find the friendly message that's in the code. Right now it's commented out, so JavaScript ignores it. Remove the comment slashes to bring it back to life.

TIP Remember, you can change the size of the JavaScript box in CodePen so you can see your code more easily. Just click the left edge of the JavaScript box and drag it over more to the left. When the JavaScript box is small, CodePen wraps long code statements and long comments over multiple lines.

Optional **Really big comments**

JavaScript has another type of comment, called a *multiline comment*. It starts with /* and has */ at the end. These comment markers have a special power. You can put them as far apart as you want. Everything in between becomes part of one massive comment.

```
/*  Everything
      in between
         the start and
         the end marker
    is part of one large comment.
*/
```

Multiline comments are useful if you want to temporarily deactivate a big section of code, or if you have a lot of information you want to write about your program in one place.

To try out a multiline comment, go back to the *Hello, Wizard!* example and remove the comment slashes (//) in front of both `alert()` statements. Now, using just one /* marker and one */ marker, disable both alert boxes. You'll know you were successful if you click the button and nothing happens. Remember, CodePen changes the text color so you can see where your comments are!

Chapter 2
How Events Work

One of the tricky things about learning JavaScript is that it's all tied up with web pages. In order to get even the simplest program to run, you need to know a bit about HTML and how an HTML element can trigger something called an *event*. Let's investigate.

A really quick HTML review

If you know HTML, you know that every web page is made out of elements. For example, the `<p>` element is for paragraphs, the `<img>` element is for pictures, the `<h1>` element is for big headings, the `<button>` element is for buttons, and so on.

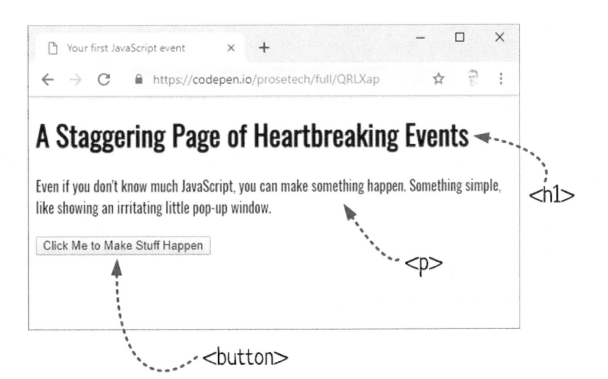

When you write a web page, all these elements seem like ordinary pieces of your web page that never change. But in the eyes of JavaScript, they're a lot more interesting. Each element pays attention to what you're doing. If you move your mouse over a picture, click a button, or start typing in a text box, JavaScript notices.

This is where events come into the picture.

How events work

JavaScript uses events to tell your code when something happens. For example, if you want to know when someone clicks a button, you can pay attention to an event JavaScript calls `onclick`.

In other words, events are the glue that connects HTML elements to your code. So how do you use them? You need to have three ingredients:

1. You need to have an element that *triggers* the event. For example, if you want your code to run when someone clicks a button, you need a `<button>` element.
2. The code you want to run needs to be in a function, like the `showMessage()` function you saw earlier.
3. You need to connect the element to the function. You do this by adding a special event attribute to your element. That's the secret sauce.

For example, imagine you have a button like this in your HTML:

```
<button>Click Me</button>
```

This is an ordinary button that says "Click Me" on it.

You want it to do something. So you write a JavaScript function that has some code, like this:

```
function showMessage() {
  alert("You clicked me.");
}
```

Now you connect the two pieces together. If you want to pay attention to the `onclick` event, you add an `onclick` attribute to the button, like so:

```
<button onclick>Click Me</button>
```

But that's still not enough! You also need to tell JavaScript which function to run. So if your function is named `showMessage()`, you write this:

```
<button onclick="showMessage()">Click Me</button>
```

Here's the computerese-to-human-language translation of what this tells JavaScript: "Pay attention to the `onclick` event. When it happens, run the code in the `showMessage` function."

> **NOTE** This part needs to be perfect. You need to match the spelling and capitalization of your function name exactly, and you need to include the empty set of parentheses after the function name. (That's your way of telling JavaScript "this here is a function.")

Try it yourself!

▶ **The Staggering Page of Heartbreaking Events (Challenge Level: Easy)**

https://codepen.io/prosetech/pen/eYZZarw

The *Staggering Page of Heartbreaking Events* has a single button. Click it, and something should happen.

Only right now, nothing does. The code you need is there, in a function named `doThatThing()`. The problem is that the button isn't connected. Can you fix it using the skills you picked up in this lesson? If you get it right, you'll see a message when you click the button.

HINT To connect your button, you need to add the `onclick` attribute to the `<button>` element, and you need to set it to the `doThatThing()` function.

Give it a try. Is it exciting? Not really! But once you have this basic setup, it opens a lot of new doorways for your exploration. One challenge you can try is to make it so that clicking the `<h1>` element (the heading) triggers the code that shows the alert box. To do this, you need to add the `onclick` event to the `<h1>` element instead of the `<button>` element.

Try it yourself!

▶ The Broken Button (Challenge Level: Easy)

https://codepen.io/prosetech/pen/xxVVNBV

The *Broken Button* gives you a slightly different version of the button event challenge. The **Click Me** button in this example is wired up to the `doSomethingAmazing()` function, but something's wrong. When you click the button, nothing happens. CodePen doesn't even show a tiny red error icon to tell you there's a problem. What went wrong?

Take a moment to investigate the web page HTML and the JavaScript code. Remember that computers don't tolerate small mistakes. If you still can't find the problem, read on for the answer.

The mistake is in the HTML. The `onclick` attribute is there, and the function name is correct. But it's missing the parentheses after the function name. Without that, JavaScript won't recognize that you're trying to use a function.

When you're making a program (in JavaScript or any programming language), even a minor typo makes the difference between working code and broken code. If there's a mistake in your JavaScript, the web browser quietly gives up as soon as it reaches the problem. Programming problems are often easy to fix—the trouble is finding them.

Chapter 3
Storing Information in Variables

Every program—small or big—needs to keep track of information. What's the user's name? What's the price of those socks you're selling? How many zombies are attacking the player every minute?

To store a piece of information, you use a *variable*.

Declaring a variable

A variable is a container with a name. You get to pick the name when you create the variable. This is called *declaring* the variable. Once you've declared it, you can put what you want inside it.

The simplest way to declare a variable is with JavaScript's `let` keyword, like this:

```
let NumberOfZombies;
```

This creates a variable called `NumberOfZombies`. Notice that you can't put spaces in a variable name, but you can use capital letters to make a variable name *look* like it has more than one word in it. Just remember that JavaScript pays attention to capitalization, so `NumberOfZombies` and `numberOfZombies` are actually two completely different names. That also means they're two completely separate containers for storing information.

Variable names can use letters, numbers (just not at the beginning), the underscore _ character, and the dash – character. But for simplicity's sake, you should probably stick to just using letters, like most other programmers.

You might wonder why JavaScript's variable-creation keyword is named `let`. The short answer is that `let` is borrowed from mathematical notation, where people say "let this variable have this value." (Also, the `var` keyword was already used in old-fashioned JavaScript. It does the same thing as `let`, but has some weird quirks, so these days people much prefer to use `let` instead.) You can think of `let` as your personal command, a way of saying "let this variable be summoned to do my bidding!"

Putting a value in a variable

To put information in a variable, you use the equal sign. Here's an example that creates a variable named age and puts the number 12 into it. This is called *assigning* a value.

```
let age;
let = 12;
```

You can think of the equal sign as being like an arrow that takes a value (from the right side) and stuffs it into a variable (on the left side of your statement).

age ← 12

You can even create a variable with `let` and assign in the same line, like this:

```
let age = 12;
```

Every variable can hold exactly one value. When you assign a value to a variable, you replace whatever was there before. Look at this example:

```
let mysteryNumber = 5;
mysteryNumber = 1;
mysteryNumber = 15;
mysteryNumber = 20;
```

What's inside the `mysteryNumber` variable when this code ends? Why, it's the number 20, of course. All the other numbers were tossed out when they were replaced.

> **NOTE** Remember, you only declare a variable once (with `let`). But you can assign a value to your variable as often as you want. The same is true of buckets—buy a bucket once, and you can change what's inside anytime.

Using numbers and text

JavaScript understands many different types of information. The two most basic types are numbers and text.

Let's take a look at three different variables that hold three different numbers:

```
let ageOfDad = 42;
let costOfSocks = 24.99;
let temperatureInSiberia = -30;
```

Notice that you can use negative numbers and decimal values. You don't use units or other symbols (like $ signs, commas, or the % percent symbol).

Now here's a variable that holds a piece of text:

```
let messageToMyEnemy = "Despair! You have coded your last variable!";
```

The text (in this case, *Despair! You have coded your last variable!*) is called a *string*. A string could have a single letter in it, some random words, or a whole paragraph.

When you create a string, you use quotation marks to show where your text starts and where it ends. You can put as much text as you want in between the quotation marks.

> **NOTE** You might wonder how you tell the difference between variables that have numbers in them and variables that have strings in them. The answer is, you don't. You just need to remember what you're doing and be consistent. (Other programming languages are more strict, and force you to say what type of data belongs in each variable you create. That strictness can help programmers avoid painful mistakes.)

Try it yourself!

▶ **Predict the Future (Challenge Level: Easy)**

https://codepen.io/prosetech/pen/KKzgzWQ

You can use a variable in any place that you'd type an ordinary number or piece of text. For example, you've already used the `alert()` function like this:

```
alert("Welcome.");
```

In this example, the text "Welcome" is an ordinary value—also known as a *literal value* (because it's *literally* what it says it is). But you can also use `alert()` with a variable, like this:

```
let welcomeMessage = "I am not at all happy to see you.";
alert(welcomeMessage);

welcomeMessage = "Please leave.";
alert(welcomeMessage);
```

Here's a question: what will these two alert boxes say? If you guessed they'll both show "welcomeMessage", you'd better try out the example for yourself.

Optional Putting quotation marks in a string

Quotation marks show the beginning and end of every text value. But what happens if you want to put an actual quotation mark inside your string? For example, what if you want to have a string that holds the text *The movie "Titanic" is my favorite*?

This won't work:

```
let favoriteMovie = "The movie "Titanic" is my favorite";
```

The problem is JavaScript assumes that the quotation mark just before the world *Titanic* is ending the string, making it just *The movie*.

The solution is to write \" instead of just " when you want to include a quotation mark inside your string. The backwards slash is a sort of secret code that gets JavaScript's attention. You can find it above the **Enter** key on most keyboards.

Here's the corrected example:

```
let favoriteMovie = "The movie \"Titanic\" is my favorite";
```

This works, but now there's another potential problem. What happens if you want to create a string with a backwards slash in it? JavaScript assumes a backward slash is the start of a secret code, so you're right back at the same problem you started with. Fortunately, there's an escape hatch. Use two backslashes in a row, like \\. Weirdly enough, that's a special JavaScript code that means "insert one backslash."

Good variable names

Plenty of disasters happen because programmers pick bad or lazy names for their variables. For example, you might be tempted to use `Number` or `num` instead of `numberOfZombies`. If you do, your code will still work, but it will be much harder for other people to understand it. (It might also be harder for *you* to understand if you forget about it for a few months and then look at it later.)

It's also important to be as consistent as possible. There are many different ways to name the same variable. For example, `AgeOfPetDog`, `ageOfPetDog`, `DogAge`, `age`, and `DogAgeInYears` are different names for the same information.

In this book, the variable and function names usually start with a lowercase letter. This is the most common style in JavaScript, but it's not universal. If you're working with a team of programmers, you might have different naming guidelines you need to follow. Otherwise, it's up to you to keep things tidy.

Try it yourself!

▶ **Hello, Ninja! (Challenge Level: Easy)**

https://codepen.io/prosetech/pen/rNeMewQ

The *Hello, Ninja!* program is as boring as you can get. It shows a message when you click a button. But right now it doesn't use any variables. You're going to change that.

Here's what you need to do:

- Declare a variable for the greeting message (let's call it `ninjaMessage`).
- Put the greeting message in the variable.
- Use your variable when you call `alert()`.

The program will still work in exactly the same way when you're finished. The goal of this example is for you to get a little bit of practice using variables before you go deeper.

Variables that don't exist

Can you use a variable that doesn't exist? That depends.

This is the right way to use a variable:

```
let welcomeText;
welcomeText = "Hello there.";
```

You can also combine *declaring* the variable and *assigning* the variable in one statement. So this code is equally as good:

```
let welcomeText = "Hello there.";
```

But this, on its own, is not good:

```
welcomeText = "Hello there.";
```

The problem is simple: It's never OK to use a variable without declaring it first with the `let` keyword.

Here's where things get a little weird. When JavaScript was first created, no one knew it was going to become so popular and important. JavaScript was built to be casual and tolerate some sloppiness. So if you try to use a variable that you haven't created, JavaScript creates it for you *automatically*. Nice, right?

Not nice.

The problem is that automatically creating variables sets you up to make all kinds of mistakes that can break your code. Like when you use a variable named `welcomeText` in one part of your program, and you use a variable named `WelcomeText` somewhere else, without realizing you've accidentally created two separate variables that have different information in them. Yikes!

To really understand this problem, you need to take a closer look in the next exercise.

Try it yourself!

▶ **Find the Impostor (Challenge Level: Medium)**

https://codepen.io/prosetech/pen/yL0aOxR

In the *Find the Impostor* example, there are three friendly ninjas ready to greet you, each with its own button. But before you click anything, check out the code, because all is not as it seems.

Right now, each ninja uses its own function. For example, if you click Kubo's button, it calls a function named greetKubo(). And that function does what you've seen before in the *Hello, Ninja!* exercise. It creates a variable, puts some text in it, and uses it with the alert() function.

But one of the ninjas is an impostor, and their greeting doesn't work. The problem is the variable mistake you just learned about in the previous section. See if you can guess who the impostor is by looking at the code. Then you can start clicking the buttons.

Give it a try now, before you read on.

Once you've found the impostor, do you know what went wrong? Can you spot the problem in the code, and correct it?

> **HINT** CodePen tries to help you spot this problem with color coding. When you declare a variable the right way, with the let keyword, the variable name turns blue everywhere you use it in your code. But variables that aren't declared stay yellow. Look at the again, and you should be able to spot the differently colored variables in Ellie's greeting.

The mistake is a small typo that accidentally creates two variables: `ellieMessage` and `elliseMessage`. You might miss the difference, but JavaScript won't. The code puts the text in `elliseMessage` but shows the empty `ellieMessage` in the alert box. You get a weird "undefined" message in the alert box because you've never assigned anything to the `ellieMessage` variable.

Once you find this problem, it's easy to fix. But it's even better if you can get CodePen to help you spot the mistake before it causes you any headaches.

One way to stop this problem is to put this magic command at the top of your JavaScript:

```
"use strict";
```

This turns on *strict mode*. To try stict mode, type this line at the top of the JavaScript box in the *Find the Impostor* example. Then click **Greet Ellie**.

Now, as soon as your code tries to use the variable that you didn't declare (`elliseMessage`), CodePen stops it. The rest of your code doesn't run, and no alert box appears. Instead, you'll get a tiny red exclamation icon appears in the bottom-right corner of the JavaScript box.

```
JS
    alert(MaoMessage);
  }

  function greetEllie() {
    var ellieMessage;
    elliseMessage = "Greetings. I am not the impostor.";
    alert(ellieMessage);
  }
```

If you click the red icon, CodePen shows a message that explains the problem in programmer language. It tells you that "elliseMessage is not defined."

```
 JS
"use strict";

Uncaught ReferenceError: elliseMessage is not defined
function greetKubo() {
  var kuboMessage;
  kuboMessage = "Why did you doubt me? For I am not the
impostor.";
  alert(kuboMessage);
}

function greetMao() {
  var maoMessage;
```

Now that CodePen has warned you about your mistake, it's much less likely to become a mysterious, head-scratching problem.

Optional Using TypeScript error checking

You don't need to copy the `use strict` command to all your JavaScript programs. Many code editors have a way to switch on strict mode in their settings. In CodePen, you can do something similar by turning on TypeScript mode.

TypeScript is a stricter version of the JavaScript language. You're not using it right now, but you can still take advantage of its automatic error checking. Here's how:

1. Click the **Settings** button at the top of the window. A new window pops up with settings for your current example.
2. Click the **JS** section on the left.

3. Click the **JavaScript Preprocessor** box, then choose **TypeScript**.
4. Click the **Save & Close** button at the bottom.

Now you'll get CodePen's red error icon whenever you try to use a variable you haven't declared, with no `"use strict"` command required.

Copying variables

You've already seen how you can put a value in a variable. But that's only the beginning. You can also copy a value from one variable to another. Here's an example:

```
let myFavoriteColor = "green";
let yourFavoriteColor = "orange";

yourFavoriteColor = myFavoriteColor;

// What is your favorite color now?
```

And here's the breakdown of what's going on:

1. The first statement creates a new `myFavoriteColor` variable and puts a value in it ("green").
2. The next statement creates a new `yourFavoriteColor` variable and puts a different value in it ("orange").
3. The third statement copies the contents of `myFavoriteColor` (the text "green") into `yourFavoriteColor`. Both of us end up with the same favorite color.

You can copy a value as often as you want. But remember, when you assign a new value to a variable, its previous contents are thrown away.

Try it yourself!

▶ **The Gift Swapper (Challenge Level: Tricky)**

https://codepen.io/prosetech/pen/bGEWjXN

For the final challenge of this lesson, you're going to try something a little bit trickier.

The *Gift Swapper* wants to help two friends, Mao and Kubo, trade gift boxes. The code is already there to get the gifts and put them in two variables. (You can ignore this code for now.)

Then the trade happens. Here's what that looks like:

```
maoGiftContents = kuboGiftContents;
kuboGiftContents = maoGiftContents;
```

But the trade-off isn't working. Can you figure out the problem? And can you fix it?

> **NOTE** Look for the comment `// FIX THIS PART` to find the gift swapping code you need to change. There's also some code in this example that uses the text boxes on the web page, but we haven't covered that technique yet.

The problem is simple enough to find. The first statement in the gift swap copies the contents of one gift box (Kubo's) to the other gift box (Mao's). From this point on, both boxes have the *same* gift. That means there's no way to get back the original contents of Mao's gift box.

> **HINT** To solve this problem, you'll need to create a third variable to help you out. That variable can temporarily store Mao's gift while you do the first part of the exchange.

Still struggling? We told you it might be tricky. Here's a breakdown of exactly how this problem can be solved:

1. Make a new variable. This is the extra box.
2. Copy the value from one gift box into the extra box. It doesn't matter which box you start with, but let's decide to move Mao's gift into the extra box.
3. Copy the value from the other gift box (that's Kubo's) into Mao's.
4. Now it's safe to take the gift out of the extra box and copy it into Kubo's box.

This picture shows you steps 2 to 4.

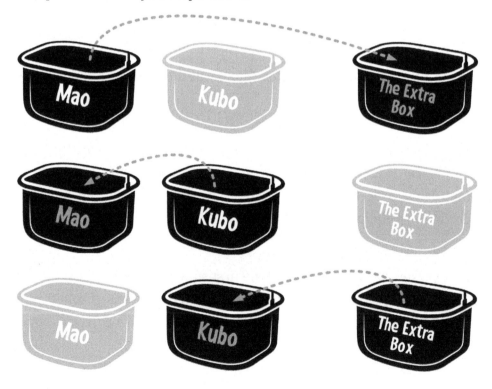

And if it still seems weird, check out the solution in CodePen.

Chapter 4

Changing Variables

Variables are called variables because their contents *vary*. In other words, you can change what's stored inside a variable as often as you want. You can rearrange bits of text, count things that happen, and perform mathematical calculations. These kinds of operations are the first step to making your code more intelligent.

Really easy math

There are lots of ways to change the value that's stored in a variable. If your variable is a number, you can use simple math.

For example, take a look at the plus + operator. It lets you add two numbers together:

```
age = 12 + 9;
```

When you run this code, JavaScript starts by doing all the math on the right side of the equal sign. In this example, that means it adds 12 and 9 to get the result (21). Then it takes that result and puts it in the age variable.

age ← 21

Of course, you can also subtract number with the - operator:

```
age = 400 - 9;

// Now age holds the number 391.
```

Both these examples have extra spaces to make the code easier to read. But if you want, you can cram everything closer together:

```
age=400-9;
```

Slightly fancier math

The + and - signs are called *operators*. JavaScript also recognizes:

- * operator for multiplication (3×2 is 3*2 in JavaScript)
- / operator for division (6÷2 is 6/2 in JavaScript)
- ** operator for exponents (6^2 is 6**2 in JavaScript)

You can also control the order that JavaScript performs its calculations with brackets ( ). Ordinarily, JavaScript follows the traditional order of operations, which means it calculates exponents first, then does multiplication and division, and ends with addition and subtraction. So if you have a statement like this:

```
total = 2+6/2;
```

JavaScript performs the 6/2 part first (it's 3), then adds 2 and 3 to get 5. Compare that to this version with parentheses:

```
total = (2+6)/2;
```

Now JavaScript adds (2+6) first to get 8, and divides that by 2 to end up with 4.

If you want to do anything more complex—like rounding numbers, or calculating exponents—you need to use JavaScript's `Math` object, which you'll explore in later lessons.

Try it yourself!

▶ **Pocket Calculator (Challenge Level: Easy)**

https://codepen.io/prosetech/pen/dyGqNGO

Here's a question. If you drive 50 mph (miles per hour) for three hours, how far do you get? But wait—don't answer this question yourself. Instead, write a statement in the Pocket Calculator program that calculates the result and puts it in the variable named `distanceTraveled`.

When you've your calculation in code, run the program. You should see an alert box pop up with the right number. (If you get 50 miles in an hour, in 3 hours you go 3×50, or 150 miles.) You can try your calculation with different numbers to see how the result changes.

Calculations with variables

Here's a useful technique: you can use a variable *in* your calculation. For example, let's say you set your age to a starting number:

```
age = 16;
```

Now you want to increase your age by one year. To do that, you take the current value of the age variable and add 1 to it:

```
age = age + 1;

// Now age holds the number 17.
```

Here's how this works. When JavaScript sees a statement like this:

`age = age + 1;`

It starts by replacing all the variables on the right side with their current values. So the statement becomes this:

`age` ← `16 + 1`

Finally, JavaScript adds up right side (getting 17), and then stuffs that back in the age variable.

Here's another example that uses division to find your equivalent age in dog years:

`ageInDogYears = age/7`

So if the age variable is 17, JavaScript evaluates this:

`ageInDogYears` ← `17/7`

And after doing the division of 17÷7, it stores the result, which works out to roughly 2.4 years:

`ageInDogYears` ← `2.428571428571429`

> **TIP** There's no limit to how many variables you can use in your calculation. But sometimes a calculation looks so complex as a single statement that it's easier to split it up into several steps.

Try it yourself!

▶ Pocket Calculator II (Challenge Level: Medium)

https://codepen.io/prosetech/pen/dyGqNGO

In this exercise you're going to perform exactly the same calculation you did in the original *Pocket Calculator* example, except now you're going to use variables. Create a speed variable and a time variable. Set them both to the proper values (50 for speed and 3 for time). Then, calculate distanceTraveled using the speed and time variables.

It may seem like a pointless change—after all, your program is still going to do the same thing. But once you start using variables you open up new possibilities. For example, instead of setting your values by typing them into the code, maybe you'll get them from some text boxes on the web page.

And using variables with good names can make it easier to understand a complex formula. Compare this:

```
distanceTraveled = time*speed;
```

To this:

```
distanceTraveled = 3*50;
```

Before you move on, try getting a little fancier with the *Pocket Calculator* example. Create a second variable, named enemyDistanceTraveled. Calculate the enemy's distance, assuming they drive for the same amount of time but at 80 miles an hour. Then, calculate how far they are ahead, and put that in a variable named gapDistance. Finally, show the gapDistance in a second alert box.

Calculations can go anywhere

Here's an interesting fact. Anywhere you put a variable, you can also put a calculation.

What does this mean? Think about the `alert()` function. You're used to calling it like this:

`alert("Hi there");`

Or with a variable, like this:

`alert(distanceTraveled);`

But you can also call it with a calculation, like this:

`alert(3*50);`

When you do that, JavaScript performs all your operations first. In this example, that means it calculates 3×50 to get 150, and then it passes 150 to the `alert()` function, which shows 150 in the alert box.

As always, your mission is to write code that makes sense. If your code seems clearer when you do everything step by step, stick to that approach. But if you're code is getting a bit cluttered up with extra variables, this kind of shortcut can help.

Really easy "math" with text

You obviously can't add and subtract letters. But JavaScript lets you do something just as useful. You can join together two separate strings to make a new one. To do that, you use the + operator, just like you do when you're adding numbers. Here's an example:

```
let firstName = "Elphaba";
let lastName = "Smith";

let fullName = firstName + lastName;
```

At the end of the code, the `fullName` variable has the combined text "ElphabaSmith" in it. Yep, what you really need there is an extra space. Here's a better attempt:

```
fullName = firstName + " " + lastName;
```

This joins together three strings: the first name, an extra space, and then the last name. The result ("Elphaba Smith") goes in the `fullName` variable.

This operation is called string *concatenation*, and it's useful in plenty of situations. For example, you can use it right now to make better, more detailed messages for your alert boxes. Here's an example:

```
let message = "It's so nice to meet you " + personName;
```

This only works if you put person's name in the `personName` variable. (You'll do that sort of thing in plenty of future exercises.) The result is a nice, personalized welcome greeting, like "It's so nice to meet you Leopold".

Adding numbers and text together

Here's an interesting dilemma. You know that if you add two numbers, JavaScript sums them up. And you also know that if you add two pieces of text (with the same + operator), JavaScript joins them to make one long piece of text. But what happens if you try to add a number to piece of text?

```
let number = 2;
let text = "4";

let combination = number + text;
```

In many other programming languages, this causes an error, because it doesn't make sense. But JavaScript is very tolerant. It assumes that you want to convert your number into a piece of text (from 2 into "2"). Then it does its text joining. The result is the longer string ("24").

Weird as this seems, it's really the only approach JavaScript can take. JavaScript doesn't try to convert your string to a number, because that might not work, depending on what's in the string. (For example, maybe your string holds a word or a sentence instead of a number. That won't make sense!) But converting a number into text *never* fails.

> **NOTE** If you want to turn a string (like "4") into a number (like 4) so you can do calculation with it, you need to perform a conversion with the handy Number() function. You'll learn that trick in Chapter 5.

Try it yourself!

▶ **Alice the Unshakeable (Challenge Level: Tricky)**

https://codepen.io/prosetech/pen/YzwjZoz

Meet Alice. She's very talkative. Once click of the **Talk to Me** button, and she'll tell you her life story, one alert box at a time.

But Alice wants a new name. (The reason is complicated. Maybe she'll explain it in her story.) Simple, right? All you need to do is find the right strings in the code, and change every occurrence of the word "Alice" to something else.

But wait. This challenge is a bit harder. Alice's new name is in a variable called `newName`. (You're going to get the new name from a text box that's on the page, but you don't need to worry about that part, because it's already working.)

To fix Alice's story, you need to use string joining and the `newName` variable. Every time she says "Alice" you need to add the `newName` variable instead. Use the + operator and pay careful attention to where you put your quotation marks!

If you've coded it right, here's a simple test. Change Alice's new name in the text box and click the **Talk to Me** button. Now Alice's story will automatically use whatever name is in the text box. Neat!

If you're having trouble figuring out this exercise, here's a line of code that demonstrates the approach you need to take:

```
alert("My name is " + newName);
```

And if you're still stuck, just click the solution link to see the whole answer.

Once you're finished, it's time to reflect. Not only did you learn to use string concatenation in this exercise, you also saw how a program can get text out of a text box. You'll learn how that trick works in the next chapter.

Optional Variables that never change

So far, every time you've needed a variable you've used the trusty `let` keyword to create it. But there's another choice. You can use `const` to create a *constant*. That's a variable that you're not allowed to change. You set it once, when you create it, and it stays that way until the function ends.

Here's an example that creates three constants:

```
const firstName = "Elphaba";
const lastName = "Smith";

const fullName = firstName + lastName;

// From this point on, you can't change firstName, lastName,
// or fullName.

// This causes an error.
lastName = "Singh";
```

At first glance, constants seem way too limited. But if you go back and look at the code you've written, you'll realize that a lot of the time you actually don't need to change your variables. For example, in the previous example, *Alice the Unshakeable*, you could use a constant for `newName`, because you set it once (when you copy the name out of the text box), and you don't change it after that.

Many people think JavaScript code is clearer when every non-changing variable is declared as a constant. That way, you know right up front that you have no intention of changing those bits of data. But in this guide, you'll stick with ordinary variables and the `let` keyword most of the time.

Chapter 5

Interacting with the Page

JavaScript was born inside a web page. People got tired of staring at ordinary HTML pages and someone said "Let's add a programming language to make things less boring!"

You've already seen how web pages run your code using events (like button clicks). But that's not the only way that JavaScript and HTML interact. Your code can *read* the information that's in the page and even *change* the page.

Introducing the DOM

JavaScript has a powerful built-in feature. It examines your web page, finds every HTML element, and automatically creates matching objects. (Objects are a special type of programming ingredient that you can use in your code.) For example, if you have a page with a paragraph and a button, JavaScript automatically creates a paragraph object and a button object. This feature is called DOM, for *Document Object Model*.

You use these DOM objects to interact with the page. For example, you can find out what text is in a text box, or change a picture, or write a message on the page. You'll learn how to do all these tasks in this chapter.

Getting information out of a text box

In many programs, you type information into a text box, and the program does something with that information. You've seen this technique in earlier exercises like *Alice the Unshakeable*.

You may already know that you make a text box using the `<input type="text">` element. Here's an example:

```
Put your name here: <input type="text">
```

That text box looks like this:

Put your name here: ▭

Now let's say you type something in the text box. How does your code get that information?

First, you need to give your text box a unique name. This name is called an `id`. Here's a text box named `nameBox`:

```
Put your name here: <input type="text" id="nameBox">
```

The `id` doesn't change how your page looks. But it gives your code a way to find the JavaScript object for your text box, and grab hold of it. And once you have the object, you can do a whole lot more—including getting the text that's inside the text box.

Here's the magic JavaScript command that pulls this off. It finds the text box and copies its text into a variable called `firstName`.

```
let firstName;
firstName = document.getElementById("nameBox").value;
```

The first statement is obvious (it creates the `firstName` variable). But the second statement needs some explanation.

Let's break it down into pieces:

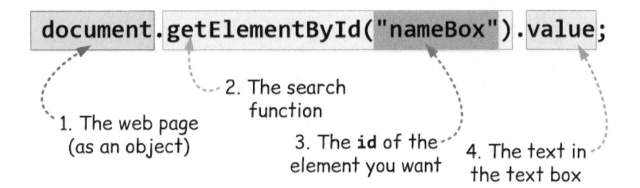

1. `document` isn't a JavaScript command. It's an object that represents the entire web page document. That means that `document` is a container that holds all the objects on your page, including the text box.
2. `getElementById()` is a function that's built into the `document` object. You use this function to search for an object with a specific `id`. The dot ties the `getElementById()` function to the `document` object.
3. `nameBox` is the `id` that you're looking for. The specific name doesn't matter, but it must match the name you wrote in your HTML *exactly*, with the same capitalization.
4. If you get all these bits right, the `getElementById()` function finds the object for your text box. The final step in this statement is to get one piece of information out of the text box object—in this case, that's the `value`, which holds its text.

The `getElementById()` function is picky. First, you need to make sure you have perfect capitalization when you call it. If you have autocomplete turned on in CodePen (as described in Chapter Zero), it will help you out by listing the functions of the `document` object as you type. If you see the match you want, just click it.

```
document.ge
}
         getElementsByTagName
         getElementsByTagNameNS
         getElementsByClassName
         getElementsByName
         getSelection
         getElementById
         getRootNode
```

As you can see, the `document` object has many more functions that can help you find objects in your web page. But you don't need to learn those right now.

When you use `document.getElementById()`, you need to make sure you type the `id` exactly right. If you make a mistake, you won't get the text box object you want. Instead, you'll get an empty value called `null`. And when you try to take the next step and get the `value` of `null`, you'll get a weird error like this:

```
Uncaught TypeError: Cannot read property 'value' of null
    var firstName;
    firstName = document.getElementById("nameDox").value;
}
```

As you spend more time with JavaScript, you'll learn to recognize `null` errors and you'll remember to check your variables and `id` names.

> **TIP** One way to avoid this sort of problem is to copy your `id` from the HTML box and paste it into your code in the JavaScript box. That way, you don't have a chance to make a mistake.

Try it yourself!

▶ A Greeting from the King (Challenge Level: Medium)

https://codepen.io/prosetech/pen/LYGMEQy

This example has three text boxes for you to fill in.

First Name:

Age:

Special Talent:

I look forward to meeting you....

[Greet the King]

The program's task is to grab this information (name, age, and special talent), and put it together to make a custom greeting from the king. (For example, if someone fills in *Wendy*, *20*, and *hiding in baththubs*, the greeting might be "Greetings, my fine squire Wendy. I've heard you are already a master at hiding in bathtubs at the ripe age of 20.")

Here's what you need to do to get this example working:

1. Give your text boxes `id` names so your code can find them.
2. Use the magic `document.getElementById()` command to get the value of each text box, and put it in three separate variables.
3. Use the + operator to build the greeting message.
4. Show the completed message with `alert()`.

Once you've finished this example, make sure you keep it around (or fork it to save it in your CodePen account). That's because you'll come back to it to make changes a little later.

Converting strings to numbers

Everything in a text box is treated like it's text. Even if you type in a number like 43298, to JavaScript it looks like a string with five characters that just happen to be digits.

Sometimes, this is a problem. For example, if you want to pull a number out of a text box and perform a calculation with it, it won't work. Remember, you can't do math with text!

The solution is to convert your string to a proper number variable. There are a few different ways to do this in JavaScript, but the most straightforward is to use a function called `Number()`. Here's how it works:

```
let someText = "42";
let myNumber = Number(someText);

// You can't do math with someText, but you can do math with myNumber.
```

In this example, the first statement creates a variable (`someText`) that holds "42" as a string. The second statement converts it to a number (42), and puts it in a second variable (`myNumber`).

It's important to realize that `Number()` only works if you have a sequence of ordinary digits. If you have something else in your string, like a comma ("42,000"), a dollar sign ("$4.14"), or some words ("84 kites"), `Number()` can't convert it. Instead, JavaScript sets your variable to `NaN`, which is a useless JavaScript codeword that means "not a number."

Try it yourself!

▶ **Broken Adder (Challenge Level: Easy)**

https://codepen.io/prosetech/pen/BajvyEb

What could be easier than adding 1+1? It turns out that it's not so straightforward when your numbers are in text boxes.

In this simple example, the code is supposed to add two text boxes. But it always gets the wrong answer. Try it out, and explain why the code is giving you such a weird result. Then, use the `Number()` function to fix it.

Showing a message in the page

So far, most of the examples you've seen have used the handy `alert()` function to show a message. That's useful when you're writing simple test programs, but it almost never makes sense in real life. After all, who wants to visit a web page that keeps popping up annoying boxes all over the place?

Instead, most web pages communicate with you by changing the page. Maybe they write a message at the bottom of the page. Or they change the color of something, or show a picture. To do any of these things, you need to use the objects in the DOM.

One of the most common page-changing techniques is writing a message in your page. The first thing you need to make this happen is an element that you can change, like a `<p>` paragraph. And once again, you need to give that element an `id` so your code can find it.

Here's an ordinary `<p>` paragraph, which is named `message`.

```
<p id="message"></p>
```

Right now this paragraph is empty. That's fine, because you're going to fill it with text using code. But it woks just as well if you put something in the paragraph to start out, and then you put something different in it with your code later on:

```
<p id="message">At the right time, a message will appear here.</p>
```

You don't need to use a paragraph. Instead, you can use any HTML element that holds text. If you want to change a bit of text inside a paragraph, it makes sense to use `<span>`. If you want to change a whole section of a page, you might use a `<div>`. And if you don't know enough about HTML to recognize these ingredients yet, don't worry—the important point is that you can change anything in your page as long as you give it an `id`.

Once again, you're going to use the `document` object with its built-in `getElementbyId()` function. But this time, you're doing the opposite of what you did before. Instead of reading information out of the page and putting it in a variable, you're going to copy information *from* a variable and put that *in* the page.

```
let newMessage = "Hello there.";

// Put the message in the <p>.
document.getElementById("message").textContent = newMessage;
```

There's one other difference between the text box example and this example with a paragraph. With a text box, you need to use the `value` property. With a paragraph, you use the `textContent` property. It's a small detail, but it's an

70

important one. To use an object, you need to know how it names its properties. (A *property* is just a variable that's attached to an object.)

Try it yourself!

> ▶ **A Greeting from the King Rebooted (Challenge Level: Medium)**

https://codepen.io/prosetech/pen/LYGMEQy

Return to the example you made for the first exercise in this section. You're going to change it to make the king's greeting appear in the page instead of in an alert box. This is a nicer approach.

To make this change, start by adding an element that will hold the message. A `<p>` makes sense, but you could use something else if you want. Don't forget the `id`!

Using the `document.getElementById()` function, and find your element. Put the message inside your element by setting the `textContent` property. Easy peasy!

Optional Changing a picture

If you become a DOM expert, you can change absolutely anything in your web page. Let's look at one more useful trick—swapping a picture.

If you know a little bit of HTML, you know that you add pictures with the `<img>` element. The `<img>` element is pretty simple. You tell it what picture to use by setting the `src` attribute with a web address, like this:

```
<img src="http://prosetech.com/tinyjs/ogre.gif">
```

Of course, if you want to change a picture in code, you also need to give it an `id`:

```
<img src="http://prosetech.com/tinyjs/ogre.gif" id="ogreImage">
```

Now you can use the same technique you've used all chapter. You search for the `<img>` object with `document.getElementById()`. Then you change the picture. This time, you make your change by setting the `src` property to point to a new address, like this:

```
document.getElementById("ogreImage").src =
  "http://prosetech.com/tinyjs/mad-ogre.gif"
```

You can tinker with this yourself if you're curious. Or, keep going to the next chapter, where you'll see an example (*The Friendly Angry Ogre*) that uses this technique.

Chapter 6
The Lifetime of a Variable

It's easy to create a variable and use it right away. But what if you want to create a variable, put something in it, and make sure it's still around the *next* time someone clicks a button?

Keeping variables alive is an important technique in programming. Imagine trying to build a game if every variable resets itself each time you click a button! But before you can take control of your variables and store information for the long term, you need to understand a bit more about how they live... and when they die.

Local variables

When you define a variable inside a function, it's called a *local variable*. It lives until the function ends. Here's an example with a string called `welcomeMessage`:

```
function sayHello() {
  let welcomeMessage = "Hi, fancy pants";

  alert(welcomeMessage);
}
```

Once the code runs and the `sayHello()` function ends, the `welcomeMessage` is thrown away, along with whatever information is inside the variable. There's no way to get that information back.

In a program, the same piece of code can run many times. For example, maybe the `sayHello()` function is attached to the `onclick` event of a button. In that case, every time you click the button this happens:

73

1. The `sayHello()` function starts.
2. It creates a new, blank copy of the `welcomeMessage` variable.
3. It puts the "Hi, fancy pants text" inside the `welcomeMessage` variable.
4. It uses `alert()` to show the message.
5. The `sayHello()` function ends, and the `welcomeMessage` function variable disappears again, taking its contents with it.

Clearly, you can't use `welcomeMessage` to store information for a longer time, because the variable only lives for a few seconds. This isn't a problem in this example, because `welcomeMessage` never changes. But there is *another way*.

Global variables

Sometimes you have a piece of information that you want to keep around for longer, maybe even as long as your program is running.

> **NOTE** In a web page, "as long as the program is running" means as long as the web page is open in the browser. As soon as you close the browser tab or go to a different page, your program is over. (In CodePen, there's one more rule—when you edit your example, the program restarts.)

To store data for a longer period of time, you need to use a *global variable*. Local variables stay in one *location* (the function where you create them). Global variables are available everywhere in your code.

To define a global variable you use the same `let` keyword, but you put it in a different place. Instead of creating your variable inside a function, you declare it *outside* of your function.

Here's an example:

```
let welcomeMessage = "Hi, fancy pants";

function sayHello() {
  alert(welcomeMessage);
}
```

You might be suspicious of this code if you remember the rule from Chapter 1 (don't put code outside a function). But code that creates variables is acceptable. It runs right away, and sets everything up for your functions to use.

> **TIP** You can put your variables before the functions that use them—or anywhere you want, really. But usually, the simplest way to organize your code is to put all your global variables at the beginning of the code file (at the top of the JavaScript box), above all your functions.

This code in this example (with the global `welcomeMessage` variable) still works the same as the earlier version (with the local `welcomeMessage` variable). But that quickly changes in slightly more complicated examples, like the ones you'll see next.

Sharing the same variable with different functions

Here's a quick recap of the two differences between global variables and a local variables:

- Local variables live until the function ends. Global variables live until the program ends—say, when you close the browser (or edit your code in CodePen).
- Local variables can only be used in one function. But you can use global variables in *every* function.

The second concept is called *scope*, and it's the one we'll explore next.

So far, you've been looking at a lot of examples with just one button and one function. But most JavaScript programs will have a bunch of functions that run when different things happen. For example, imagine you have a three-button program like this:

When you click **Become Nice**, it sets `welcomeMessage` to something nice:

```
function beNice() {
  welcomeMessage = "I'm so delighted you could join me for tea.";
}
```

When you click **Become Mean**, it sets `welcomeMessage` to something else:

```
function beMean() {
  welcomeMessage = "I plan to eat you and your pet goldfish.";
}
```

When you click **Say Hello**, you get whatever greeting you last chose:

```
function sayHello() {
  alert(welcomeMessage);
}
```

In the next exercise, you can try creating this example.

Try it yourself!

▶ **The Friendly Angry Ogre (Challenge Level: Medium)**

https://codepen.io/prosetech/pen/mdVzpNg

In this example you start out with three buttons (Become Nice, Become Mean, and Say Hello). There's also a tiny bit of code that changes the picture to match the ogre's mood.

The part that's missing is the message you're going to show. To make this example work, you need to set the right message, depending on the ogre's mood. Then you need to show this message at the right time.

Here's what you need to do:

1. Create the `welcomeMessage` variable. Remember, it needs to be a global variable, and you only need to define it once.
2. Add the code that sets `welcomeMessage` when **Become Nice** or **Become Mean** is clicked. You need two different messages, depending on what mood you've put the ogre in.
3. Add the code to `sayHello()` that shows the message.

What happens if you click **Say Hello** without clicking **Become Mean** or **Become Nice** first? Can you give `welcomeMessage` a starting value so this doesn't happen? (A good starting value for an ogre with no mood is a message like "I just don't know how to behave.")

Try it yourself!

▶ **The Broken Jellybean Counter (Challenge Level: Medium)**

https://codepen.io/prosetech/pen/PoZyQPo

If there's one thing programmers like to do, it's counting things. (If there are two things programmers like to do, it's counting things and eating jellybeans.) That makes this next example the perfect bit of practice.

The Broken Jellybean Counter lets you eat as many jellybeans as you want—just click a button each time you want to eat one. It counts the number of jellybeans you've eaten so far.

Unfortunately, there are two disastrous mistakes in the program. Can you fix them?

> **HINT** Right now, the bean counter uses local variables. But you need to turn `beanCount` into a global variable, so you can use it everywhere. Make that change, and you're well on your way to solving the problem.

The secret of the braces

I have a confession to make. Earlier, I said that local variables live until the function ends. That's true, but it's not the whole story.

Technically, local variables live in the block that contains them. As you might remember from Chapter 1, a block is a common structure in JavaScript code. It's any section of code that fits between two braces { }.

So far, all the braces you've seen have been for functions. However, in the upcoming chapters you're going to learn that you also use braces to group together code for different reasons. For example, you use braces to repeat code in a loop, or make it conditional. If you create a variable inside one of these sections, it doesn't live for the whole function. It only lives until that *block* is finished.

This will all make more sense when you see examples of the other ways we use braces. But here's a cheat rule that always works—when you create a local variable, it will disappear from existence when you reach the next } closing brace.

Wise advice about global variables

The more global variables you use, the more difficult it is to figure out what's going on in your code. Imagine you see a new JavaScript program for the first time, and it has a bunch of global variables. How do you know which functions use which variables? There's no way to be sure without reading all the code, and that means there's plenty of room to make a mistake.

To make your code as simple as possible, and to reduce the chance of making mistakes in the future, you should use global variables only when you need them to share information.

Sometimes, you might notice in your program that different functions are using the same local variables for the same tasks. For example, maybe you have three functions and each one creates its own local `welcomeMessage` variable. It might occur to you that you could replace these three local variables with one global `welcomeMessage` variable. Don't do it! It's always better to make your functions as independent as possible.

Chapter 7
Making Decisions

So far your programs have been a little short in the brains department. The key ingredient they're missing is the ability to *make decisions*—in other words, to evaluate information and then set a course.

To add this ability, you need to learn a programming concept called *conditional logic*. It's the art of asking questions, and then choosing what to do.

Introducing conditions

A condition is a question that has two possible answers: true or false.

For example, look at this condition with two variables:

```
a > b
```

This condition makes a simple claim: *a is greater than b*. If a holds the number 12, and b holds the number 3, this condition is true. But if a holds the number 3, and b holds the number 12, this condition is false. (This condition assumes that a and b are numbers. If they aren't, this condition doesn't make sense.)

Here's another example of a condition:

```
a == b
```

This condition asks *does a equal b?* In this case, it doesn't matter what type of data the variable a holds—it could be a number or a piece of text. The important part is that the variable b has exactly the same content as a. So if they both hold the same number (like 42) or a matching piece of text (like "blunderstone"), the condition is true.

You might be wondering why there are two equal signs (==). That's just the way JavaScript works, because it wants to distinguish between = (which you use to set a variable) and == (which you use to compare values in a condition). Some other programming languages use the ordinary = for both uses.

The if statement

To get a condition to actually do something, you need to pair it with the `if` keyword. Here's an example:

```
if (a > b) {
  // (Do something here.)
}
```

The `if` statement tells JavaScript to look at a condition and run a piece of code if the condition is true. Here's how it breaks down:

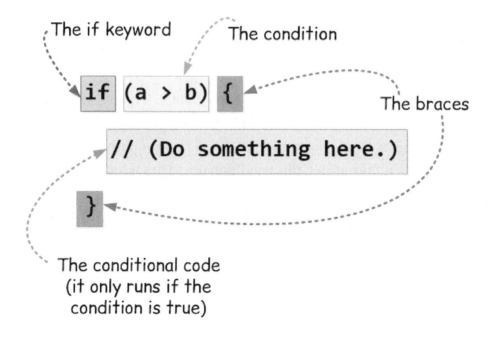

Remember, a condition can only have two possible outcomes:

- If the condition is true (in this example, a is greater than b), JavaScript runs the code between the two braces.
- If the condition is false (a is less than or equal to b), JavaScript skips over the code in the braces and carries on.

You can put as many lines of code as you want in between the braces. They all become part of the same conditional block. If you only need a single code statement in your conditional block, you can remove the braces. But we recommend always keeping the braces to make your code clearer.

Can you tell what happens in this next example?

```
alert("Hi");

if (a == b) {
   alert("They match");
}

alert("Bye");
```

The condition in this example checks if two variables have the same value. If they do, you'll get a sequence of alert boxes (*Hi*, then *They match*, and finally *Bye*). If a and b hold different variables, you still get the *Hi* and *Bye* boxes, but the code in the `if` block is skipped.

When you write an `if` block, make sure to remember the parentheses around your condition, or it won't work. Here's a common mistake:

```
// Where are my parentheses?
if a == b {
```

And don't make this mistake:

```
// This is the wrong equal sign.
if (a = b) {
```

A single equal sign is only good for *setting* variables. So this code actually copies the value from b into a, which definitely isn't what you want.

More logical operators

The symbols < and > and == are called *logical operators*, because you use them to compare values in a condition. They are the most common logical operators, but there are still a few more to learn.

Instead of asking if two variables are equal, you can ask if they are *not equal*. This is exactly the opposite question. You do this by changing the == in your condition to !=

```
if (a != b) {
   alert("Nope, no match");
}
```

This condition asks "do these variables have different values?" If they do, the condition is true and the alert box appears. Otherwise, there's no message.

You can also use the >= (greater than or equal) and <= (less than or equal) operators, which work like > and < except they are also true when your two numbers are the same.

Here's a quick review of all the logical operators, with an example for each one:

Operator	Name	Example Condition	Result When a=10
==	Equal to	(a == 10)	true
!=	Not equal to	(a != 10)	false
<	Less than	(a < 10)	false
<=	Less than or equal	(a <= 10)	true
>	Greater than	(a > 10)	false
>=	Greater than or equal	(a >= 10)	true
===	Equal in value and type (so no variable conversion allowed)	(a === "10")	false
!==	Not the same value or not the same type	(a !== "10")	true

The === and !== are two more specialized operators. They're included to give you the complete list, but you won't use them anytime soon.

> **NOTE** You already know that <= is a combination of < and = that means *less than or equal*. You might think you could write it the other way around, with the equal sign first, like =<. But JavaScript doesn't recognize it that way, and you'll get an error if you try.

Try it yourself!

▶ **The Bowl of Beans (Challenge Level: Medium)**

https://codepen.io/prosetech/pen/OJMrEXq

Who doesn't enjoy a bowl of jellybeans?

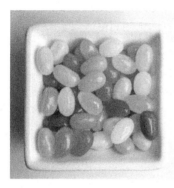

You have 19 jellybeans left.

[Eat One] [Fill Bowl]

This example lets you take jellybeans out of your bowl one at a time, or fill the bowl back up (by clicking buttons, of course). The code keeps track of how many jellybeans are in the bowl. But there's a problem. No one stops you from taking a jellybean, even if there are none left. That leads to an embarrassing problem—run the program long enough, and you'll have a negative number of jellybeans in the bowl.

To avoid this problem, you need to add an `if` block. The idea is that you should only allow a bean to be taken from the bowl if there's at least one remaining. Otherwise, don't do anything.

> **HINT** If you're stuck, start by writing the condition you want to test. How do you know if the bowl is empty? You could use the condition `jellybeanCount >= 1`, which checks if there is one or more beans in the bowl. Or, you could use the condition `jellybeanCount != 0`, meaning the bowl has *not* dwindled down to 0 jellybeans. Either way, use that condition with an `if` block, and put the code for eating the jellybean inside.

Keep this program around. You're going to come back to it in a moment.

The else block

The `if` statement has a trusty companion called `else`. If you use `if` to set up a conditional block of code, you can use `else` to tell your program what to do if the condition *doesn't* match.

The easiest way to understand `if` and `else` is with an example:

```
if (a == b) {
   alert("They match");
}
else {
   alert("They don't match");
}
```

Your program can take *only one* path through an `if else` block. In this example, if the first condition matches, you get the first alert box message. If it doesn't, you get the second alert box message. There's no way to see both messages, and there's no way to skip them both either.

This kind of arrangement looks complicated, but it's very useful. It allows your code to choose between different outcomes, which is important when you're examining information or playing a game of chance.

> **NOTE** Before, you used braces for one thing—functions. Now you're using them for functions and conditional logic. Make sure you remember to put braces at the beginning and end of each block of conditional logic, and at the beginning and end of your entire function. It's fairly common to forget a brace, at which point your code will stop working. To help spot the problem, use indenting in your blocks.

Try it yourself!

▶ **The Bowl of Beans Improved (Challenge Level: Easy)**

https://codepen.io/prosetech/pen/OJMrEXq

You can improve the Bowl of Beans example by adding an `else` statement. Right now, there's a single all-or-nothing test that checks if the bowl is empty. But here's a better way to serve the jellybeans:

- If there are beans in the bowl, dish one out (as usual).
- If there are no beans left in the bowl, show an alert box explaining the problem.

Conditional logic with unlimited possibilities

First you started with one conditional block. Then you used `else` to combine two blocks. Now you'll learn a technique that lets you stack an unlimited number of conditions, one after the other.

The secret is a combination called `else if`. You use `else if` to consider another condition. But here's the trick: `else if` only checks its condition if the previous condition didn't match.

The easiest way to understand how this work is to look at a couple of examples. First, consider this code, which has two separate conditions:

```
if (moneyInWallet > 0) {
   alert("You are carrying some money.");
}

if (moneyInBank > 0) {
   alert("You have money in the bank.");
}
```

This code has several possible outcomes.

- If you are totally broke (no money anywhere), you won't see any alert messages.
- If you have money in both your wallet and the bank, you'll get two messages.
- If you have money in just one place (wallet or bank), you'll get one message.

But when you use `else if`, you can link your conditions, like this:

```
if (moneyInWallet > 0) {
   alert("You can buy something!");
}
else if (moneyInBank > 0) {
   alert("You can buy something, if you go to the bank first.");
}
else {
   alert("Maybe ask your parents for some bills?");
}
```

When JavaScript runs this code, it checks the conditions in order. As soon as it finds a condition that's true, it runs the code in the corresponding block. It then skips over all the other `else` statements, going right to the closing } at the end.

This system means you always see exactly one message in this example:

- If you have money in your wallet, you get the first message.
- If you have no money in your wallet, but you do have money in the bank, you get the second message.
- If you have no money anywhere, you get the third message.

You can use as many `else if` blocks as you want. Their conditions can use the same variables or different variables (like in the wallet and bank example). Just remember that as soon as one condition matches, the others are ignored.

You don't need to have a final `else` block at the end. But if you do, that code runs if none of the other conditions match.

Try it yourself!

▶ **Predict the Future (Challenge Level: Easy)**

https://codepen.io/prosetech/pen/mdVvdxV

Take a look at this block of conditional logic, which has three separate condition and a final `else`.

```
if (a == b) {
  alert("They match");
}
else if (a < b) {
  alert("A is smaller than B");
}
else if (a > b) {
  alert("A is bigger than B");
}
else {
  alert("I can't compare them. They aren't numbers.");
}
```

Your goal is to run the code in your mind. Try to predict what will happen for the following values of a and b:

Value of a	Value of b	Result
42	5	
239.12	239.12	
0	100.5	
4	"dog"	

Once you've made your predictions, try out the actual program and see if you're right. If not, what was your mistake?

Try it yourself!

▶ Beans Ain't Free (Challenge Level: Hard)

https://codepen.io/prosetech/pen/jOWXKwb

Here's a more advanced version of the jellybean bowl counter. Now the code keeps track of two changing numbers: the amount of jellybeans in the bowl (`jellybeanCount`) and the amount of money you have (`moneyInWallet`). And whenever you fill the bowl, the jellybean cost is deducted from your wallet automatically.

The problem is that there's no code to check that you actually have the money you're spending. That means a few too many button clicks can put you deep into debt, with a negative amount of money. Jellybeans may be good, but they aren't worth a lifetime of financial hardship.

To fix this code, change it so it does this when you click the **Fill Bowl** button:

1. Check if your bowl is full. If it is, no more beans will fit anyway, so show a message explaining the problem.
2. If your bowl has room, see if you have money to fill the bowl. If you don't show a message explaining *that* problem.
3. If the bowl has room and you have money, fill the bowl up to the maximum 20 jellybeans and deduct the usual fee.

> **HINT** To solve this puzzle, you need to create a multipart `if` block in the `fillBowl()` function. First check if condition 1 from the list above fails (or 2, because the order doesn't matter). Then, use an `else if` to go ahead and check if the other condition fails. Finally, use an `else` to tell the program what to do if neither condition failed. (This is where you put the current code that buys more beans.)

Chapter 8
More Decision Making

The `if` and `else` keywords give you everything you need to make decisions in your code. But sometimes conditional logic can get messy. You decide to check one variable, then another, and the next thing you know your code is buried somewhere in a wall of braces { }.

Don't panic. You can learn to write code that makes decisions but keeps the confusion under control. Here are some tools that can help.

Combining two conditions (using 'and')

A conditional block of code is like any other block of code. Inside it, you can create variables, show alert boxes, and interact with the page. You can even put one `if` block inside *another* `if` block, like this:

```
// I don't want to spend more than $10 for a pineapple.
if (costOfPineapples <= 9.99) {

  // But wait, do I even have enough money?
  if (moneyInWallet >= costOfPineapples) {
    // Everything checks out. Time to buy one.
  }

}
```

This example begins by checking the cost of pineapples. If it's more than $9.99, the program skips over the entire conditional block and the example is finished. But if it's less than $9.99, the program enters the conditional block, where it performs a *second* test. This test checks if you have enough money to buy the fruit you want. If that's also true, the program enters the second conditional block.

This example works fine, but there's another, more compact way to write the same example. It looks like this:

```
if (costOfPineapples <= 9.99 && moneyInWallet >= costOfPineapples {

  // Everything checks out. Time to buy one.

}
```

Now both conditions are fused together into one test, using the && symbol, which means *and*. In other words, the code in this block only happens if the cost of pineapples is low enough *and* if you have sufficient money.

So is this example better than the first version? It depends. If you want to write some code that runs if pineapples are cheap, *no matter what's in your wallet*, then you need to use the first approach. (For example, maybe you want to tell someone about the low price, and then make your decision about whether to buy any.) But if you only need code that runs when both conditions are true (cheap pineapples *and* full wallet), then using && makes your code more compact and easier to read.

> **NOTE** You might wonder why JavaScript uses the && symbol to mean *and*. The truth is that this is just the way that the JavaScript language is designed. It matches other finicky-syntax languages like C, C#, and Java. But some other languages, like Visual Basic and Python, use the actual word and instead of a symbol. (If you're having trouble finding the & key on your keyboard, hold down **Shift** and press **7**.)

You can and use && to combine even more than two conditions. In fact, you can combine as many as you want, just keep adding && to the end, followed by your new condition. Just remember to keep it all in between the parentheses.

```
if (a != 0 && b !=0 && a > b && b < c) {
  // a is not 0, b is not 0, a is greater than b,
  // and b is less than c.
}
```

Combining two conditions (using 'or')

When you use && you ask *Are both these conditions true?* You can also ask *Is at least one of these conditions true?* For that you need the || symbol, which means *or*.

```
if (costOfPineapples < 9.99 || costOfMangoes < 0.99) {
  // As long as one of these fruits is cheap enough,
  // it's worth a trip to the store.
}
```

When you use ||, just one of your conditions needs to be true to run the conditional block.

Don't confuse | with an L or I character. Technically, | is the pipe symbol. On most keyboards you type it by holding down **Shift** and typing the backslash \ (which you'll find under the backspace key somewhere to the right).

Here's a table that summarizes how conditions are combined with *and* and *or*:

Operator	If the first condition is...	And the second condition is...	Result
&&	true	true	true
	true	false	false
	false	true	false
	false	false	false
||	true	true	true
	true	false	true
	false	true	true
	false	false	false

Try it yourself!

▶ **Predict the Future (Challenge Level: Medium)**

https://codepen.io/prosetech/pen/WNrmQzR

It's time to turn yourself into the JavaScript engine and run some mental code. Take a look at this block of conditional logic, which uses && and ||. It's a little trickier than it seems.

```
if (a == b && a > 0) {
  alert("You reached door 1");
}
else if (a != 0) {
  alert("You reached door 2");
}
```

```
else if (a > b || b == 0) {
  alert("You reached door 3");
}
else {
  alert("You reached door 4");
}
```

Try to predict what will happen for the following values of a and b.

Value of a	Value of b	Result (what message you see)
42	5	
5	5	
0	0	
0	42	

Once you've made your predictions, try out the actual program and see if you're right. Did you remember the rule of else if—you only get the *first* matching condition? That means you'll only see one alert box.

This example is designed to exercise your brain. When you write conditional logic, it shouldn't look like this. Instead, you should take the effort to make your conditions clear and predictable. If it's simpler to split your conditions apart and write more if blocks, do that.

The switch statement

When you use the if statement, your code can become a bit long-winded. JavaScript has another way to write conditional logic that's more compact. It's the switch statement.

The `switch` statement is a more limited version of `if`. It only works if you want to examine just one variable. For example, if you plan to ask the question "what day of the week is it today?" and you want to write conditional code for each day, the `switch` statement works great. But if you want to compare different combinations of variables, as in the previous example, `switch` isn't much help.

> **NOTE** There's nothing that `switch` can do that `if` can't do. So why bother to use `switch`? It's really a matter of your own taste, but if `switch` works for you, you'll usually get shorter, tidier code than you would with `if`.

To use switch, you start by presenting the variable you want to examine, like this:

```
switch (dayOfTheWeek) {
```

Now you write conditional code for the different values. Each one of these is a separate *case*, and you identify them with the `case` keyword.

```
case "Saturday":
```

In the `dayOfTheWeek` example, you're expecting one of seven different day names. Each value is in quotation marks because it's a string. If you use `switch` with a variable that holds a number, you wouldn't use quotation marks.

After you write `case` and put the value you're looking for (like "Saturday" or 478), you add a colon : to start your conditional code.

```
case "Saturday":
    alert("It's Saturday. Time to write some JavaScript!");
```

You can write as many lines of code as you want for each case, but you need to write break at the end.

```
case "Saturday":
  alert("It's Saturday. Time to write some JavaScript!");
  break;
```

This is different than JavaScript's usual way of organizing things. Instead of putting your conditional code between braces, you start it with : and end it with break.

You can also write one bit of code that deals with several cases. To do that, you stack the cases on top of each other, like this:

```
case "Tuesday":
case "Wednesday":
case "Thursday":
  alert("It's the middle of the week. Keep waiting");
  break;
```

Here's the complete days of the week example with switch:

```
switch (dayOfTheWeek) {
  case "Saturday":
    alert("It's Saturday. Time to write some JavaScript!");
    break;
  case "Sunday":
    alert("It's Sunday. Last day to write some JavaScript!");
    break;
  case "Tuesday":
  case "Wednesday":
  case "Thursday":
    alert("It's the middle of the week. Keep waiting.");
    break;
  case "Friday":
    alert("Almost there...");
    break;
}
```

Try it yourself!

> ▶ **The Goblin Dice Gambler (Challenge Level: Medium)**

https://codepen.io/prosetech/pen/pogGGOg

Did we convince you that using `switch` can be faster than using `if`? In this exercise, you'll get to see the difference for yourself. You're going to take a prewritten game about a gambling goblin and rewrite its `if` block to use `switch` instead.

You can't beat *me* at a game of chance!

Roll 'Em Good!   Try Again

You lost $150. You now have $4.

Before you get started, take a moment to figure out how the code is organized. You'll find more than one conditional block in this example. The first section of conditional code checks the number that you rolled. This is the part you need to change. (The other section of conditional code figures out if you've won or lost the game.)

Once you've finished your work, you can enjoy the rest of the program. Who knows, maybe you'll even make a few changes of your own!

If you look closely, you'll find a couple of tricks you haven't seen before.

First, the code "rolls" the dice by getting a random number. That needs the help of a special object called `Math`, and you'll learn all about it in Chapter 13.

Second, the code sets the dice picture to match the number you rolled using a variation of the picture-changing trick from Chapter 5. For example, if you roll a 3, the code turns that number into the picture file *dice3.png*. Put that in an `<img>` element, and you get the picture that shows the dice roll. Not too shabby!

Chapter 9
Repeating Yourself with Loops

Computers never get tired. If you give them a job, they keep at it until it's done. If you want to calculate a formula, they don't care whether it's once or a thousand times in a row. And in this chapter, you'll see just how easy it is to make your code do something a thousand times in row. All you need is a *loop*.

The simplest possible loop

JavaScript has several different types of loops. All of them share one thing in common—you put the code you want to repeat in between braces { }.

Here's a simple example with something called a `while` loop:

```
// Don't try this at home.
while (true) {

   alert("Welcome to Groundhog Day.");

}
```

The `while` keyword starts the loop:

```
while
```

Immediately after that are the parentheses ( ) where you put a condition. The condition tells the loop when to end.

```
while ()
```

In this example, the condition is just `true`, which means the loop never ends.

```
while (true)
```

After the condition are the braces { } that hold the code you want to repeat.

```
while (true) {

}
```

So what does JavaScript do when it meets a loop like this? Here's a breakdown:

1. JavaScript checks the loop condition.
2. If the condition evaluates to true, JavaScript starts the code in the loop.
3. JavaScript runs all the code statements in the braces from top to bottom. In this example, there's just one code statement in the loop. It shows an alert box with a message about Groundhog Day.
4. JavaScript returns to the first step and starts the process over.

As long as the condition is true, JavaScript keeps re-running the code in the loop. In this example, the condition stays true *forever*, which means a new alert box appears every time you close the last one. (But remember, the `alert()` command pauses your code until you click OK. That means you'll never see more than one alert box box pop up at the same time.)

This never-ending sequence of alert boxes lasts until you end the program by closing the browser tab or refreshing the page.

A loop that counts

A loop that carries on forever is called an *infinite loop*. In a real program, you would never create an infinite loop on purpose. Instead, you'd use a condition that eventually turns false, ending the loop and letting JavaScript continue to the rest of your code.

The simplest approach is to make a loop that runs an exact number of times. You decide how many times the loop should repeat its code, and you use a variable to enforce it.

For example, you might create a variable named `counter`:

```
let counter = 0;
```

It's important that you create this variable *before* the loop, not *inside* the loop.

You use your counter to keep track of what's happening. Each time the loop runs its code, you add one to your counter. Basically, you're counting the number of times the loop repeats.

The counting code goes in the loop:

```
counter = counter + 1;
```

The final ingredient is a condition that tells the loop when to stop. For example, you might tell JavaScript to repeat the loop while the counter is less than 10:

```
while (counter < 10)
```

When a loop ends, JavaScript continues to run whatever code is after the loop.

Proper counting is important. People sometimes get tripped by the fact that most counters start at 0, or they're not sure whether to use < or <=. But you don't need to take my word on it. Try this next example to see for yourself how many times a loop repeats.

Try it yourself!

▶ **Predict the Future (Challenge Level: Easy)**

https://codepen.io/prosetech/pen/qBNygyg

Here's a loop that shows alert boxes. It creates a variable named `counter` to keep track of how many times it goes around the loop:

```
let counter = 0;

while (counter < 10) {
  counter = counter + 1;
  alert(counter);
}
```

Your challenge is to run the code in your brain. Go line by line, one loop at a time, to figure out what's going to happen. What sequence of alert boxes will you see before the code ends?

Now try changing the < to <=. What changes?

Try it yourself!

▶ **Put It In Reverse (Challenge Level: Medium)**

https://codepen.io/prosetech/pen/qBNygyg

The most common type of counter is one that starts at 0 and continues upward. But JavaScript doesn't limit you. For example, you could make a counter that increases by fives. Or, you could create a counter that counts down from a maximum value.

Your next challenge is to revisit the ordinary loop you saw in the previous exercise, and switch it around. Make it count down from 10. However, make sure you see the same number of alert boxes as you did before. (Obviously, the order of the alert boxes is going to be reversed.)

There's more than one way to solve this problem, but all the solutions are similar.

> **HINT** There are two changes you need to make a count-down loop. You need to change the statement that changes the counter. Instead of increasing it by 1, you need to *reduce* it by 1. You also need to change your condition so that it keeps going while the counter is above 0.

Putting the condition at the end

Most programming languages have more than one type of loop, and JavaScript is no exception. You've just learned about the `while` loop, which makes this the perfect time to tell you about the very similar, but slightly rearranged, `do while` loop.

Here's the `do while` version of the 1-to-10 counting loop you saw before:

```
let counter = 0;

do {

  counter = counter + 1;
  alert(counter);

} while (counter < 10);
```

As you can see, the `do while` loop puts the condition at the *end* of the loop. It also adds a semicolon (`;`) after the condition, which is another weird detail you just need to remember.

Although the do while loop looks a little different than the earlier example, it has the same effect. That probably makes you wonder—why is there another way to code the same loop? The answer is that sometimes the do while loop *does* have a different result than the while loop. Here's why.

When you use do while, JavaScript runs your code and checks the condition *at the end* of each loop. That means that no matter what condition you use, your loop code runs at least once. Compare that to the ordinary while loop, which checks its condition up front. If the condition starts out false, the while loop skips over the loop completely. It doesn't even run it once.

Here's a demonstration of the difference:

```
let data = 0;

while (data == 1) {
  // This code never runs, because
  // the condition starts out false.
}

do {
  // This code runs one time, even though
  // the condition is false.
} while (data == 1);
```

The difference is easy to see—but what's the point?

It turns out that sometimes it's more convenient to use the do while structure in loops that don't have counters. You'll see an example in the Million Dollar Pizza exercise later in this chapter.

A loop without a counter

So far, you've seen a few examples of loops that use counters. Loops with counters keep track of how many times they repeat, and they pull the plug at just the right time.

But sometimes you don't know exactly how many times your loop should loop. For example, maybe you're using a loop to create an animation, and you want to stop after a certain amount of time. Or maybe you're using a loop to run a game, which ends when someone reaches a certain amount of points. Or perhaps you're performing a series of calculations, and you're not going to stop until you find a certain value. In cases like these, you need to write a different type of condition for your loop.

Just to get you thinking, here's a rough example of how the code in a game might work, with all the messy details left out:

```
do {

    // (Play one round of the game here ...)

    // (Increase the score of the winner here ...)

    // Use the condition to stop when someone gets 50 points.
} while (playerOneScore < 50 && playerTwoScore < 50);

// Yippee, we have a winner!
// If you reach this point, someone has 50 points or more.
// Now you can use an if block to find out who won.
```

Ready to take on some actual code? Try the next exercise, where you get to use a loop to make yourself a million dollars.

Try it yourself!

▶ **Million Dollar Pizza (Challenge Level: Medium)**

https://codepen.io/prosetech/pen/XWKJQYz

Don't you hate when this happens? You borrowed half a million dollars so you could start a pizza business. (Dreams, right?) But can you pay it back before you go bankrupt?

There's just one more thing. The money ($500,000 in cold, hard cash) came from a mob boss that isn't in a particularly generous mood…

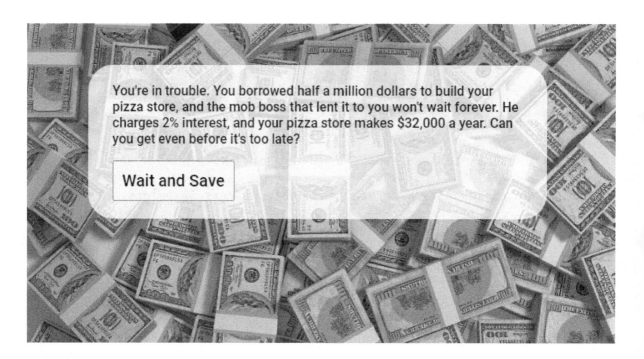

To figure this out, you need a loop that will calculate the money you owe, and the money you're making, every year. If you save up enough to pay your debt, you can end the loop, pay back the loan, and ride off into the sunset.

Here's how the calculations work. Every year you're charged 2% interest. You can use that to calculate how much you owe:

```
amountOwed = amountOwed * 1.02;
```

So if the `amountOwed` starts at 500000, after the first year it grows to 510000. And so on.

But at the same time, your pizza shop is making money, to the respectable amount of $32,000 per year. You can track your growing savings using a formula like this:

```
amountEarned = amountEarned + 32000;
```

Each pass through the loop represents one year of time passing. At the end of the loop, you must use a condition to test if you've earned enough to pay off the amount owned. If you have, end the loop, and tell us how many years it took. Easy, right?

> **HINT** Your condition needs to compare `amountOwed` to `amountEarned`, You need to keep track of the number of years in the loop (by adding 1 each time the loop runs), but you don't use the `years` variable in the loop condition.

Try it yourself!

> ▶ **Million Dollar Pizza II (Challenge Level: Hard)**

https://codepen.io/prosetech/pen/NWrBZWg

If you want to show off, here's another challenge that builds on the first version of Million Dollar Pizza.

First, try the original program (the one you wrote in the last exercise) using different amounts of money or interest. Play around long enough, and you'll notice a big problem. If the amount you owe is growing faster than the amount you make, the loop you wrote becomes an infinite loop. That's because there's no way to pay off the loan, no matter how many centuries you take. But computers can miss obvious facts like this, and your page gets locked up trying to save your store and looping forever.

Your next challenge is to adjust the code to set a timeout. In other words, after a number of years the mob boss comes to collect. If you don't have enough money by this point, and you lose.

Here's how to build this solution:

1. You need a new condition that ends the loop when a certain number of years has passed (say, 30).
2. Join the new condition to your first condition with the && symbol (meaning *and*, as described in Chapter 8). That way your loop keeps going as long as you need more money, *and* you haven't reached deadline.
3. After the loop ends, use an `if` block to figure out what happened. Check if you have enough money. If not, you must have hit the deadline, so show a different message.

The full solution is in the example project, if you need it.

Optional For, a loop with a built-in counter

If you haven't had quite enough loop-y goodness yet, JavaScript has another tool for you. It's called the for loop.

A for loop is basically a loop with a built-in counter. If that's what you need, you'll find that for is more compact than while, though it doesn't add any new features.

Here's an example. You probably remember this loop of messages from the first exercise in this chapter:

```
let counter = 0;

while (counter < 10) {
  counter = counter + 1;
  alert(counter);
}
```

With a for loop, it looks like this:

```
for (let counter = 0; counter < 10; counter++) {
  alert(counter);
}
```

After the word for is a set of parentheses with three important details, separated by semicolons. The first part creates the counter:

for (**let counter = 0;**

The second part sets the condition that's tested before each pass:

for (let counter = 0; **counter < 10;**

And the third part changes the counter, in this case by adding 1 to it using the ++ operator:

for (let counter = 0; counter < 10; **counter++**)

When you use a for loop, it's obvious that the variable in your parentheses is the counter. So, rather than name it counter, lazy programmers usually give it a much shorter name. Traditionally, they choose i, although the exact name doesn't matter:

```
for (let i = 0; i < 10; i++) {
  alert(counter);
}
```

Anything you can do with for you can also do with while, But in real life, when people need a counter they almost always use a for loop.

Chapter 10

Organizing with Functions

There's a pattern in all the examples you've seen so far. You click a button, and a function springs into action. Every once in a while you add *another* button to your page, and then you use another function to deal with its clicks.

As your programs become more complicated, it's important to organize your code. One of the ways to do that is by making more functions, and breaking your logic down into smaller pieces.

Adding new functions

Most of the programs you've seen so far have had just one function, which runs when you click a button. But there's nothing stopping you from making more.

To add a function, all you need is the `function` keyword, followed by the function's name, empty parentheses ( ), and a set of braces { }.

```
function doSomething() {
}
```

Function names follow the same rules as variables names, which don't allow spaces and special characters (other than underscores _ and dashes –). Usually, the first letter of a function name is lowercase. And it's never OK to give two functions the same name.

Check out this example with three functions:

```
function doSomething() {
  // There's nothing going in here right now.
}

function showMessage() {
  alert("Greetings from the showMessage() function.");
}

function showAnotherMessage() {
  alert("Welcome to the showAnotherMessage() function.");
}
```

You can put functions in any order you want. The order you write them has no effect on the order that they're used in your program. But it's important to always remember your braces. A common mistake is forgetting to end a function with a closing }, so that two functions blend together in a pile-up of code that JavaScript can't understand.

Calling a function

You already know that you can connect an event to a function. To do that, you set an event attribute in your HTML. For example, if you want to handle the `onclick` event of a button, you might set it like this:

```
<button onclick="doSomething()">Click Me</button>
```

This works because `doSomething()` is actually a valid line of JavaScript. So when the `onclick` event happens, all it needs to do is run this statement, which calls the `doSomething()` function.

If you understand that, it will come as no surprise to find out that you can call a function in your own code using the same technique.

For example, check out this revised version of the `doSomething()` function, which calls *another* function:

```
function doSomething() {
  showMessage();
}
```

Now when someone clicks the **Click Me** button, it triggers the `doSomething()` function, and the `doSomething()` function calls the `showMessage()` function. The `showMessage()` function uses `alert()` to show a message letting you know what's going on.

This process is known as *calling* a function. Here's what happens when you click the **Click Me** button:

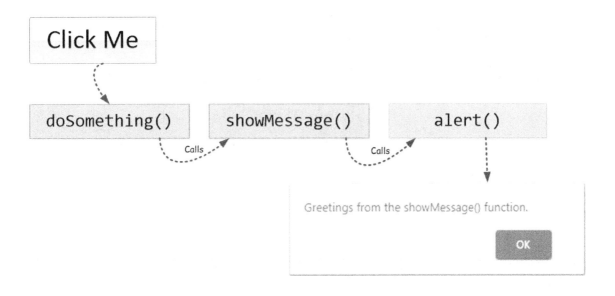

It's easy to recognize when code is calling a function, because there are always a pair of () parentheses after the function name. You can't call the `showMessage()` function like this:

```
showMessage;     // What does it even mean?
```

You call a function whenever you want. You can even call more than one in a row:

```
function doSomething() {
```

```
  showMessage();
  showAnotherMessage();
}
```

When you call a function, JavaScript lets that function do all its work before it carries on. In this example, that means JavaScript runs all the code in `showMessage()`, and *then* runs the code in `showAnotherMessage()`.

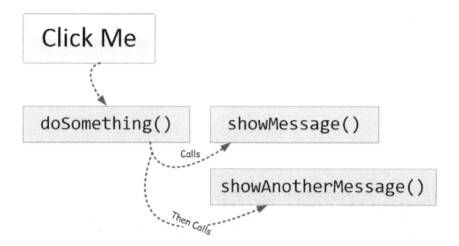

If calling more than one function in a row isn't exciting enough, you can also make a function that calls another function, which can then call another function, and so on. This isn't as complicated as it sounds. In a well-designed program, every function does one separate task, and the function name usually tells you what that task is.

Imagine you read code like this:

```
function doSomething() {
  checkPassword();
  saveOrder();
  goToCheckoutPage();
}
```

It's pretty clear what the `doSomething()` function is accomplishing, even without digging in to all the code in the other three functions it calls.

Try it yourself!

> ▶ **Follow the Function Trail (Challenge Level: Easy)**

https://codepen.io/prosetech/pen/WNrYyYR

In a real program, you'll find piles of functions. When the program is running, JavaScript jumps from one to another, and you'll need to be able to follow along.

This exercise gives you the chance to think like engine by following a trail of function calls. Start by looking at the code (but don't run it). The program has two buttons, and each one calls a different combination of the same functions. On a piece of paper, write down the order of messages that you expect to see for each button. It's trickier than it seems, because some functions call other functions, and so on. Then, run the program to see if you're right.

The point of this exercise is just to see how functions work. In real life, your functions aren't one-liners showing messages. But once you know how to call a super-short function, you know how to call a longer one, because they work exactly the same.

Also, checking the assumptions you have about your code is a Programmer Life Skill. Often, weird errors happen because your code isn't doing what you think it's doing.

Here's a final test you might want to try. What happens if you call a function that calls itself? Or if function A( ) calls B( ) which then calls A( )?

Functions that get data

As you've already seen, every time you call a function you put a set of parentheses ( ) after the function name. These aren't just for decoration. They also allow you to send one or more pieces of data to a function. Each piece of data is called a *parameter*.

In order for this technique to work, your function must be designed to accept parameters. Plenty of functions are. One example is the alert() function that you've used many times. You send the message you want it to show using a string:

```
alert("Hello from the alert function.");
```

To make a function that accepts parameters, you need to declare them. For example, look at this simple no-parameter version of the showMessage() function:

```
function showMessage() {
  alert("Greetings from the showMessage() function.");
}
```

To add a parameter, you put it in between the parentheses after the function name:

```
function showMessage(guestName) {
  alert("Greetings from the showMessage() function.");
}
```

Adding a parameter is just like defining a variable. In fact, the guestName parameter *is* a variable—it's a container that will hold the data that gets sent to the showMessage() function. The only difference is that you don't use the let keyword.

Now, when you call showMessage() somewhere else in your program, you can supply the guestName data:

```
function doSomething() {
  showMessage("Alexa");
}
```

This example sends a string containing "Alexa" to showMessage(). It you have a variable that holds a string, that's just as good:

```
function doSomething() {
  let name = "Alexa";
  showMessage(name);
}
```

Of course, you need to know what type of data the function wants. Is it a number? A string? Are there values that aren't allowed? This is a topic that gets much more important when you start making bigger programs and working with other programmers. Often you can put comments before the function declaration to explain these details. But that's a conversation for a later time.

There's still something missing in this example. Right now, the doSomething() function sends the string to the showMessage() function, which successfully receives it and puts it in the guestName variable. But the showMessage() function doesn't actually use this bit of information. That's easy to change:

```
// showMessage() shows a personalized message in an alert box.
// guestName is the name of the person using the program.
function showMessage(guestName) {

  alert("Greetings, " + guestName +
    ", from the showMessage() function.");
}
```

Now, if you call this slightly enhanced function with the name "Alexa" you'll get the message "Greetings, Alexa, from the showMessage() function."

Using multiple parameters

The trusty alert() function takes just a single parameter, and so does the revised showMessage() function you just saw. But if you want to make a function that has two parameters, it's easy. You just need to add two parameter names and separate them with a comma:

```
function showMessage(firstName, lastName) {
  alert("Hello Dr. " + lastName + ". Can I call you " +
    firstName + "?");
```

}

Now when you call this version of the showMessage() function, you supply two pieces of information:

```
showMessage("Alexa", "Chen");
```

What message will the showMessage() function show?

You can keep adding as many commas and parameters as you want. Just remember that order is important. The order that you list your parameters in the function declaration is the same order you need to follow when you call the function.

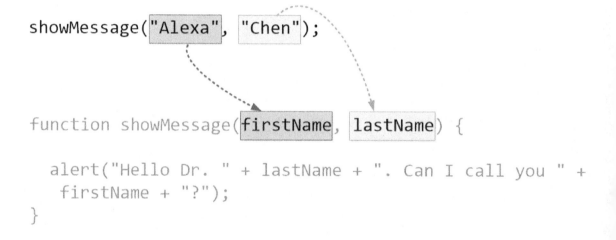

Try it yourself!

▶ **Alien Language Translator (Challenge Level: Medium)**

https://codepen.io/prosetech/pen/rNLQmgw

A new alien race has arrived on planet Earth. They appear to be friendly, but understanding each other is difficult. You think you can make yourself understood, but you're going to need a JavaScript function to help you communicate.

Your first job is to translate an ordinary string of text into alien language. You type your message into the text box. Then, when you click the button, it's time to translate it.

Right now, clicking the button calls the `speakToAlien()` function, which doesn't do anything (because there's no code in it). Your job is to get the text out of the text box, and then translate it.

Getting the text is easy, if you remember how. First, check the HTML to find out what `id` the text box uses (in this example, it's `message`). Then, create a variable and use the trusty `document.getElementById()` function, like this:

```
let messageToTranslate;
messageToTranslate = document.getElementById("message").value;
```

Once you have the text, you need to convert it to alien language. But you don't need to translate it on your own. Instead, there's *another*, already written function in this page called `convertEnglishToAlien()` that can do the job.

The `convertEnglishToAlien()` function uses one parameter, called `message`. This allows you to send the text you want to translate to the function. If you do this correctly, `convertEnglishToAlien()` will show the super-weird translation in an alert box. Try it out!

In the next chapter, you'll get to use an even better alien translation function.

Chapter 11
Functions that Answer Questions

In the last chapter, you saw how functions are like building blocks. You (or someone else) writes them. Then you call your functions into action whenever you need them.

Now it's time to build smarter functions that can give you information. With their help, you can organize your code and even reuse the best stuff in different programs.

Functions that give answers

One common job for a function is to give you a piece of information. For example, you might call a function that performs a special calculation and gives you the answer. The information that the function sends back to you is called a *return value*.

Every function can have one return value. You use the `return` command to provide the return value. For example, if you want your function to send the number 10 back, you could add this statement to your function:

```
return 10;
```

But there's a catch. As soon as you use `return`, the function ends. JavaScript doesn't run the rest of the function's code (if there is any).

Here's a more realistic example. The `addTwoNumbers()` function takes two numbers (through parameters) adds them, and then returns the result.

```
function addTwoNumbers(firstNumber, secondNumber) {
  let sum = firstNumber + secondNumber;
  return sum;
}
```

Clearly, you don't actually *need* a function to do this job, but the concept is the same if you make a more sophisticated function. For example, here's a version of addTwoNumbers() that adds a little frill. If you give it numbers in strings (like "3" and "5") it still works, because it translates the text to real numbers:

```
function addTwoNumbers(firstNumber, secondNumber) {
  let sum = Number(firstNumber) + Number(secondNumber);
  return sum;
}
```

In the next chapter you'll use the Math object, which has lots of functions that give you answers. For example, Math.Sqrt() function to get the square root of a number.

So how do you use a function that has a return value? You could just call it normally:

```
addTwoNumber(42, 6);
```

But if you do this, you'll never see the return value. For some functions, that might make sense, but for addTwoNumbers() it defeats the purpose. If you want to store the return value in a variable, you need to assign it using the equal sign. Here's an example:

```
let sum;
sum = addTwoNumbers(42, 6);
// Now sum holds the value 48.
```

When JavaScript runs this statement, it calls addTwoNumbers(), sends the two parameters (42 and 6), gets the result, and finally copies that sum into the result variable.

Try it yourself!

▶ Predict the Future (Challenge Level: Easy)

https://codepen.io/prosetech/pen/mdEaJJq

You can use a return value anywhere you would ordinarily put a variable. For example, you could use it in a calculation:

```
result = addTwoNumbers(42, 6) + 10;
```

What will result be after this statement? If you're uncertain, check your answer with the sample page.

You can also use a return value in a condition:

```
if (addTwoNumbers(4, 6) > 10) {
}
```

Will this be true?

You can even use a result value as a parameter to another function call:

```
alert(addTwoNumbers(450, 1));
```

What do you expect to see when you run this code?

Try it yourself!

> ▶ **Alien Language Translator II (Challenge Level: Hard)**

https://codepen.io/prosetech/pen/MWedawx

In the first version of the Alien Language Translator exercise, you learned to call the `convertEnglishToAlien()` function and send it two parameters. But there's a tiny flaw.

Right now, the `convertEnglishToAlien()` function takes your message, performs its alien-language conversion, and shows the result in an alert box. But what if you want to do something else with your alien message? Maybe you want to show it on the page, or pass it to another function.

A perfect version of `convertEnglishToAlien()` would let you decide. It would stick to its one job: translating English to alien. You'd send it some information (through parameters), it would send you back the result (through the return value), and *then* your code would decide what to do with the message.

This is your new job—change the `convertEnglishToAlien()` to use a return value. Here's what you need to do:

1. Remove the code that shows `scrambledMessage` in an alert box.
2. Add a statement at the end of `convertEnglishToAlien()` that returns `scrambledMessage` using the `return` keyword.
3. Now change the code that calls `convertEnglishToAlien()` so that it takes the return value and assigns it to a new variable (call it something like `translation`).
4. Finally, add some new code to show the translation on the page. Remember, this code doesn't go in the `convertEnglishToAlien()` function. Instead, you use it right *after* you call `convertEnglishToAlien()`, when you get the return

value. (In the sample code, you'll see the logic to is already partly there, and it's marked with a comment.)

Once you've solved this problem, there's another improvement you can make to the Alien Language Translator.

So far, you've been changing the code for the **Translate To Alien** button. But this exercise also has a **Translate To English** button and a matching function called `convertAlienToEnglish()`. Right now, the **Translate To English** button does nothing. You need to write the code that gets the text from the alien text box, passes it to `convertAlienToEnglish()`, and then shows the result in the English text box. You'll need to write this code yourself, but it's very similar to the code for the **Translate To Alien** button.

As a bonus, if you finish the job successfully, you'll be able to decode the alien's mysterious first words.

Chapter 12
Getting More Serious with Math

You already know how to do basic calculations with numbers, like addition and subtraction. But as your programs get more ambitious, you'll need more math skills.

For example, if your code works with decimal values, you need to know how to round them to the right size before you show them in a page. Or maybe you want to perform calculations with exponents and square roots, use trigonometric identities (like sine, cosine, and tangent), or use the mathematical constant pi (π). JavaScript has built-in features for all of this mathematical wizardry.

Math shortcuts

One of the most common mathematical operations in a program is changing a variable. Here's an example:

```
counter = counter + 1;
```

As you can probably tell, this statement takes the counter variable, adds 1, and assigns that as the new counter variable.

This sort of operation is so popular that JavaScript gives you a shortcut with the += operator:

```
counter += 1;
```

Did you catch that? The += operator tells JavaScript to take the variable on the right side of your statement (in this example, that's 1), and add it to whatever variable is on the left.

This trick also works if you want to paste a bit of text onto the end of a string:

```
let message = "Let's eat";
message += " some panckes";

// Now message holds the text "Let's eat some pancakes."
```

JavaScript has similar shortcuts for subtraction, multiplication, and division. They all work the same, but the + part of the += operator is replaced with the type of mathematical operation you want to do:

```
let counter = 12;

counter -= 2;
// (Now counter =12-2, which is 10.)

counter /= 5;
// (Now counter =10/5, which is 2.)

counter *=3;
// (Now counter is 6. You know why.)
```

There's really nothing special about using a shortcut like += instead of writing out a full statement with = and +. But it does let lazy programmers save a few keystrokes. You don't *need* to use it, but you'll see it in other people's programs.

There's one other shortcut you might come across: the ++ and -- operators. They adjust a variable by adding or subtracting 1, with no equal sign required.

```
let counter = 10;

counter++;
// (Now counter is 11.)

counter--;
// (Now counter is 10 again.)
```

The -- and ++ operators exist because changing a variable by 1 is very common job in code. This shortcut is so famous it's what the C++ language is named after. (Although C++ lets you use it to skip around in memory, which is a trickier and riskier operation.)

Try it yourself!

▶ Predict the Future (Challenge Level: Easy)

https://codepen.io/prosetech/pen/pobKJLV

If you understand how the +, ++, and += operators work, you should be able to solve this puzzle pretty quickly.

```
let a = 10;
let b = 10;
b = a + b;
b -= b/2;
b++;
b += a;
b *= 10;
b--;
```

This code doesn't change a. But what happens to b by the time you reach the end?

133

The wacky mistake JavaScript makes with decimals

It's time for some bad news. Computers have a weird way of dealing with decimal values.

You already learned that JavaScript numbers are very flexible. You can use a number variable to store an integer (like -342) or something bigger (like 8093411059) or more precise (like 0.00000345908). This is called a *floating point* number, because the decimal "floats" around to make numbers as big or small as you need.

Computers have quick and efficient ways to store floating point numbers and perform calculations with them. However, there's a catch. Certain decimal values aren't stored with perfect precision. As a result, you can get bizarre rounding errors in your calculations. The rounding errors are very tiny, but they can still make a mess.

To see the problem, try the Dime Adder example at https://codepen.io/prosetech/pen/JjGVBVa. Each time you click, it adds $0.10 to a running total that's shown in the page. This works for the first couple of clicks, but when you expect to get to $0.30, you'll instead get the number 0.30000000000000004. Add some more dimes, and things go back to normal—untl you'll reach 0.7999999999999999 when you should have $0.80 cents. Clearly something is wrong.

Your change purse holds: $**0.30000000000000004**

Add a Dime

The problem is that some decimal values can't be translated exactly into floating point numbers. (It's similar to the problem you face if you try to write 1/3 as a decimal value. You can write 0.33333 with as many 3s as fit on your sheet of paper, but it's still not a perfect representation of a third.)

This problem isn't just with JavaScript. It happens with floating point numbers in every programming language. The difference is that some languages have decimal data types that are designed to avoid this problem. JavaScript doesn't, so it's up to you to correct the mistake.

How do you fix it? If you're writing a program that uses scientific calculations with lots of decimal places, there's no need to change anything. But if you're writing a program that uses exact amounts of money, it's confusing to see tiny fractions of a penny.

There are two solutions. You could use rounding, which you'll learn how to do in a moment. That way you can snip off any extra decimal bit that doesn't make sense. But an easier approach is to avoid having decimal values at all. So instead of keeping track of an amount of dollars (like $4.30), count the total number of cents (like 430).

Try it yourself!

> ▶ **The Broken Dime Adder (Challenge Level: Medium)**

https://codepen.io/prosetech/pen/JjGVBVa

It's confusing when you see tiny rounding errors in money amounts. Try this program, and confirm that the problem exists once you add a few pennies. Then, fix the issue by replacing the `dollars` variable with a `cents` variable that counts the total number of pennies (and doesn't need decimals). Remember to change your number of cents back to a number of dollars before you show it in the page.

Peeking into the Math object

If you own an ordinary scientific calculator, you know it doesn't just add, subtract, multiply, and divide. There are plenty more features crammed into special buttons. JavaScript is like that, too. The basic math functions are built into the JavaScript language with the operators you've already learned about (+-*/^). But when you need more calculating power, you turn to a special feature called the Math object.

The Math object bundles together a bunch of functions that do specialized math calculations. You can take a peek at all them when you're writing code. Type Math, followed by the period (.), and you'll see a list of everything the Math object offers.

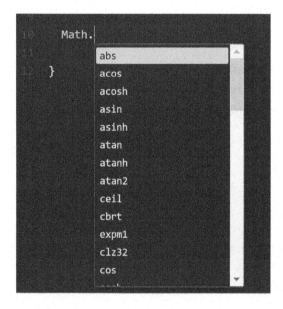

All of these functions take one or more parameters, and give you the result as a return value.

For example, if you want to calculate the square root of a number, you can use the `Math.sqrt()` function. (Here, `Math` is the object and `sqrt()` is one of its functions.)

```
let number = 9;
number = Math.sqrt(number);

// Now number holds 3 (because that's the square root of 9).
```

The `Math` object isn't just about square roots. If you want to calculate the tangent of an angle (important in high school trigonometry, and in games where projectiles fly through the air), you can use `Math.tan()`. And so on.

Try it yourself!

▶ **How Big Is this Cake? (Challenge Level: Medium)**

https://codepen.io/prosetech/pen/QWyRYjQ

Few problems are as important as the one you'll tackle in this challenge—measuring exactly how big a cake you're about to eat.

Cake diameter (inches): 8

How Big Is this Cake?

The area is: 50.26548245743669 inches squared

If you remember a bit of geometry, you might know how to calculate the area of a shape. For a simple rectangle, you need to multiply its length and width. For a circle, you perform a similar but more complex calculation that looks like this:

$$\pi (d/2)^2$$

In this equation, *d* is the diameter of the circle and *pi* (π) is the magic mathematical constant that starts with 3.14 and continues on forever. But you don't need to remember the digits of *pi* yourself, because the Math object has a built-in variable that stores it for you.

Take a moment to see if you can find *pi* in the Math object. Then use it to calculate the area of your cake. You need to write a statement that divides the diameter by 2, squares the result, and then multiplies that by *pi*. You can do it all in one line of code, or you can break it down into a separate steps if you think that's easier. Remember that you need to use the ** operator for exponents (4**2 means 4^2).

> **NOTE** Math.PI acts like a variable. That means you don't need to use parentheses like you do when you use one of the built-in Math functions.

Rounding numbers

If someone asks you how big your cake is, it's reasonable to say 8 inches. It's less helpful if you tell them 8.045840982 inches. But JavaScript is like that.

In your code, it doesn't matter if numbers have a long decimal portion, like 8.045840982. You can keep using it in calculations like any other value in a variable. But if you want to *show* your number somewhere, like in an alter box or on the web page, you'll probably want to trim it down to a tidier size.

The Math object has a round() function that can do the job. Here it is chopping all the decimals off a number:

```
let longNumber = 4.349;
let roundedNumber = math.Round(longNumber);

// Now roundedNumber is 4
```

The round() function always rounds to the nearest whole number. So 4.349 becomes 4 and 4.931 becomes 5. But what if you want to round to a different digit?

For example, let's say you want to keep exactly two decimal digits, so 4.349 becomes 4.35. You might expect that the round() function could do this for you, but it's not that helpful. You need to work for it.

In this situation, you need to juggle your number around with a bit of multiplication and division. Here's a demonstration:

```
let longNumber = 4.349;

// Move the decimal to the right two places.
longNumber = longNumber * 100              // longNumber=434.9

// Round the number.
let roundedNumber = math.Round(longNumber);    // roundedNumber=435

// Move the decimal back where it was before.
roundedNumber = roundedNumber / 100        // rounderNumber=4.35
```

This example moves the decimal to the right place, rounds the number, and then moves the decimal back where it was before. Once you get used to this pattern, you can combine it all it a single statement:

```
let longNumber = 4.349;
let roundedNumber = math.Round(longNumber*100) / 100;
```

Try it yourself!

▶ **How Big Is this Cake? (Challenge Level: Easy)**

https://codepen.io/prosetech/pen/QWyRYjQ

The cake calculator doesn't leave out any decimal places, and that makes its measurements a bit scary. But you can fix the problem using the `Math.round()` function. You don't need to keep any decimal places, so you won't even need to multiply the total cake area before you round it to a more manageable whole number. Easy!

Chapter 13
The Magic of Random Numbers

If you've ever rolled a pair of dice, flipped a coin, a picked a piece of paper out of a hat (with your eyes closed!) you understand the idea of randomness. When you play these simple games, the result is up to chance. You can't predict what will happen.

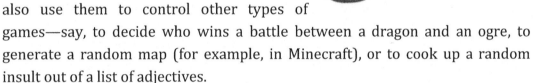

In programming, you get the same effect using random numbers. Random numbers let you simulate games of chance, like rolling dice and drawing cards. You can also use them to control other types of games—say, to decide who wins a battle between a dragon and an ogre, to generate a random map (for example, in Minecraft), or to cook up a random insult out of a list of adjectives.

In this lesson, you'll use random numbers to make two basic games.

Random and pseudo-random

Being random isn't easy for a computer. (It's about as difficult as getting a robot to laugh.) When you ask a computer to give you a random number, it actually follows some kind of not-so-random formula to create a "fake" random number (technically called a *pseudo-random* number). For example, it might look at the computer clock, take the millisecond at that exact moment, and feed it into some sort of mathematical formula.

One benefit of this approach is that your computer can pick fake random numbers pretty quickly. And in your program, the numbers still *seem* completely random, because you never know what number your computer will pick. But if you're trying to use a random number in computer security—for example, to encode sensitive information or to pick the winner in the next megamillion dollar lottery—this is a problem. Hackers can figure out how you're generating your fake random numbers, guess them, and crack open your data (or give themselves winning loto tickets).

Fortunately, you don't need to worry about that if you're building an ordinary game in JavaScript.

Generating random numbers

Like most programming languages, JavaScript has a way to create a random number. You use the `Math.random()` function:

```
let randomNumber = Math.random();
alert("You random number is " + randomNumber);
```

If you run this code, you'll find that the random number probably isn't what you expect. Maybe you want a random number between 1 and 6 (representing the roll of a dice). What you actually get is a massive fractional value that's more than 0 but less than 1, like this:

```
0.43085308054
```

It's random, but not very helpful. It's up to you to take this fractional value and convert it to a number in the range you want.

Here's the good news. There's a formula you can use to pick a random whole number. The formula looks like this:

```
randomNumber = Math.floor(Math.random() * (max - min + 1) ) + min;
```

It looks complicated at first, but it breaks down easily. First, you need to understand all the ingredients. The `min` is the minimum number you allow, and max is the maximum number. So if you're trying to pick a number between 1 and 6, the formula becomes:

```
randomNumber = Math.floor(Math.random() * (6 - 1 + 1) ) + 1;
```

Now we can simplify it a little:

```
randomNumber = Math.floor(Math.random() * 6) + 1;
```

This calculation uses two new `Math` functions: `Math.random()` and `Math.floor()`.

`Math.floor()` is a specialized rounding function that always rounds down, cutting off the decimal portion of a number. For example, if you use `Math.floor()` on the number 4.839424982, it becomes 4. (JavaScript also has a matching `Math.ceil()` function that always rounds up.)

You don't need to understand how this statement works its magic in order to use it. But if you want to know what's going on, let's take a second look at the final formula:

```
randomNumber = Math.floor(Math.random() * 6) + 1;
```

Here's a step by step breakdown of what JavaScript does when it runs this statement:

1. `Math.random()` gets a random value that's more than 0 and less than 1.
2. You multiply that by 6, turning it into a random number that's more than 0 and less than 6. However, the decimal part is still there, so you'll have a number like 4.839424982.
3. `Math.floor()` chops off the decimals and leaves you with a whole number. That number could be 0, 1, 2, 3, 4, or 5.
4. You add 1 to shift your range of numbers up one place. Now you've got a whole number from 1 to 6, which is exactly what you want!

Try it yourself!

▶ **Number Guesser of Doom (Challenge Level: Medium)**

https://codepen.io/prosetech/pen/JjXPWJr

In this exercise you need to complete the number guesser game. You have all the concepts you need, but there are quite a few details to fill in.

NUMBER GUESSER OF DOOM

I am thinking of a number between 1 and 10.

Guess my number in 4 tries or be **CRUSHED**.

First, look at the code. You'll see two global variables at the top:

```
let secretNumber;
let numberOfGuesses = 0;
```

Your first job is to pick a secret number between 1 and 10. You want to pick this number once, store it in `secretNumber`, and keep the same number for all your guesses.

The best time to pick the secret number is when the page first loads. To do that, you can write a function that reacts to the `onload` event. The number guesser already has function connect to the `onload` event of the `<body>` element:

```
<body onload="pickNumber()">
```

Right now, there's no code in the `pickNumber()` function. Your first job is to pick a random number here using `Math.random()`, and store it in `secretNumber` for later.

Once you've got the number picking under control, the next job is to handle the guesses. To guess, you fill a number in the text box and click the **Guess** button. This triggers the `guess()` function.

The `guess()` function already has the code to get grab the guess out of the text box. Now you need to use conditional logic to test if the guess matches the secret number. You can then show a congratulations message (for success), or a taunting insult (for failure). You can show your message on the page—in fact, the code is already there. All you need to do is set the `message` variable with the right text.

Once you get to this point, try out the example and make sure it works. When everything is in place, it's time to finish your example with some important extra details:

1. Keep track of the number of guesses using the global `numberOfGuesses` variable.
2. After a wrong guess, check if you've reached the maximum number of guesses (4). If you have, show a "game over" message (and tell the guesser what the number was).
3. After every guess, say how many guesses are left. You can add this information to the end of the message you show.
4. After losing the game, reset `numberOfGuesses` to 0, and pick a new random number. You don't need to write your random logic again—instead, just call the `pickNumber()` function.

If you complete all these tasks, you will have a truly epic number guessing game.

Try it yourself!

> ▶ **Ice, Dagger, Lava (Challenge Level: Tricky)**

https://codepen.io/prosetech/pen/rNeByow

If you've ever played rock, paper, scissors, you'll have no trouble understanding the number one gaming hit in the goblin kingdom: *Ice, Dagger, Lava*. In each round, you and your opponent choose to use ice, a dagger, or the lava of an erupting volcano. Here's how you decide who wins:

1. Lava melts the dagger. (Winner: lava)
2. Dagger breaks the ice. (Winner: dagger)
3. Ice hardens lava into stone. (Winner: ice)

If you both choose the same attack, no one wins.

The *Ice, Dagger, Lava* code is already set up with most of what you need. You click one of three pictures to choose your attack. Then, the `playIceDaggerOrLava()` function decides who wins. Your job is to write the code for that function.

Your opponent is a computer goblin, who chooses an attack at random. Choosing between three options is the same as choosing a random number from 1 to 3. For example, you could ice is 1, dagger is 2, and lava is 3. To make that system easier to remember, the code use three constants:

```
const ice = 1;
const dagger = 2;
const lava = 3;
```

Remember, constants are just variables that never change.

The button clicking code is already there. For example, if you click the ice picture this is what happens:

```
function pickIce() {
   playIceDaggerOrLava(ice);
}
```

Calling `playIceDaggerOrLava(ice)` is the same as `playIceDaggerOrLava(1)`. But if you use the constant names in your code instead of the magic numbers, your code is easier to understand, and you're less likely to mix up a number.

Now it's time for your contribution. You need to write the code in `playIceDaggerOrLava()`. First, you need to pick a random number from 1 to 3, representing ice, dagger, or lava. That's the easy part.

Now you need to write an `if` block that figures out who wins. This part is tricky because there are many ways to win and many ways to lose. The best approach is to use a two-part strategy. First, you figure out whether it's a win or a loss, and *then* you decide what to do about it.

There are many different ways to solve this problem. Some are shorter than others, and some look more complicated. One option is to use a variable to store the result:

`let result;`

If it's a win, you something in `result` (like the number 1). If it's a loss, you store a different value. After you've tried all the different ice, dagger, lava combinations, you can check `result` to decide what to do next.

The last step is the easier part. If the player won, show a happy win message. If not, show something less kind.

There are lots of ways to make this example even better. Why not use a couple of variables to keep track of how many games you win and lose? You can then show than information somewhere else on the page, and even use it to calculate a win percentage.

What Comes Next

If you liked this introduction to JavaScript, the journey doesn't need to end here. We've got a sequel planned for the future.

Meet *A Tiny Introduction to Object-Oriented JavaScript*. It takes you on a new adventure—learning to build your own objects. What's an object, you ask? It's nothing less than one of the most practical programming tools ever invented, and something you'll use in plenty of other programming languages.

To find out when new books are released (and when there's updated content for this book), sign up for Tiny Introductions news at http://tiny.cc/tinyintro. You can also follow me on Twitter (http://twitter.com/prosetech), or just say hi at matthew@prosetech.com!

Until then, happy travels,

Matthew

Made in United States
North Haven, CT
20 March 2022